Fighting for Deliverance

Idemudia Guobadia

CONTENTS

ACKNOWLEDGMENTS AND DEDICATION

It is my pleasure to dedicate this book to my Lord and Savior, Jesus Christ. He is the One who brought me out of deep darkness and despair, and I remain eternally grateful. I owe Him everything, and I pray that this book will always be for His glory.

I cannot fail to appreciate my wonderful wife, Temitayo, for her love, patience, understanding, and support for all the time I needed to be alone to write this book.

Special thanks also go to Shannon Ray Davis of Omega Man Radio and Pastor Kay Boachie of Fresh Fire Prayer Ministry for inspiring me to keep on writing.

Special thanks also to all my co-laborers in Christ at Overcomers in Christ Faith Assembly, Brooklyn, New York.

Idemudia Guobadia
Newark, NJ
March 2016

FOREWORD

By Pastor Kay Boachie

Fighting for Deliverance by Pastor Idemudia Guobadia is a great book for spiritual warfare and deliverance. This book is intended for anyone genuinely seeking for true deliverance the biblical way. This manual will equip every Christian soldier and minister of the gospel of Jesus Christ who would like to know how to wage a good warfare against the kingdom of darkness. In spiritual warfare and deliverance, you cannot effectively fight and be delivered from an enemy you are ignorant of or know very little about. Your ignorance of the devil and his devices will cause him to gain advantage over you and hold your health, finances, marriage, family, and destiny in bondage. In *Fighting for Deliverance*, Pastor ID discusses how the devil is systematically gaining advantage over many areas of our lives because of our lack of knowledge about his devices. Remember that ignorance is one of Satan's greatest weapons.

This book will help you to gain spiritual insight, knowledge, and a better understanding of the devil and his devices used to ensnare people so that you can avoid his traps and deceptions. You will be empowered with biblical weapons needed to fight for your deliverance and win the battle against the powers of darkness. You will not only learn steps to take to receive your deliverance, but also how to maintain your deliverance once you have received it from our Lord Jesus Christ.

Within these pages, Pastor ID—who was once an occultist and is now saved and delivered by Jesus Christ—exposes the deceptions and devices the devil uses to keep people in bondage. With his wealth of knowledge from the satanic kingdom, he is better able to teach you how to discern the strategies of the devil and how to overcome the devil. You will learn how to fight for your deliverance until you are completely free from the yoke of bondage.

I have personally been blessed by the topics discussed in this book. It gave me a better understanding as a deliverance minister why we do what we do when administering deliverance to people. I gained a lot of understanding and knowledge from reading *Fighting for Deliverance*. I applaud the effort of Pastor ID in writing this book. He has allowed himself to be used by God to help set the body of Christ free from the bondage of the devil.

Fighting for Deliverance is a much-needed manual for this adulterous generation, who are under the control of the devil and his cohorts. I highly recommend that everybody get a copy of this book and gain knowledge and understanding about the devices of the devil in these last days.

Pastor Kay Boachie (Brother Kay)
Fresh Fire Prayer Ministry

1

DELIVERANCE FROM FALSE TEACHING AND DECEPTION

There is a danger of being misled by so many false teachings and doctrines that resemble the true teachings of Christ. To avoid this snare of deception, you must be thoroughly grounded and rooted in the Word of God. You must make it a habit to always be learning and knowing the Word of God contained in the Holy Bible. If you do not know the truth or if you become careless with the truth, it will be easy for Satan to convince you that a lie is the truth. You must know the Word of God, and the church you belong to must systematically teach His true and unadulterated Word. Christ admonishes the true believer to hold on to His teaching:

> To the Jews who had believed him, Jesus said, "If you hold to my teaching, you are really my disciples. Then you will know the truth, and the truth will set you free" *(John 8:31–32)*.

The pure truth is embodied in Christ's teachings. It is this truth that delivers. Here, Christ states clearly that he has his teachings. Every other teaching that is not of Christ is a false one. The test for determining whether a teaching is true or false is to examine it in the light of the Holy Bible. Christ has spoken often in parables and in deep spiritual language that has raised various interpretations regarding the truth. Let's consider the following example:

In John 3, Jesus Christ has a conversation with Nicodemus. Christ informs Nicodemus in John 3:3 that except a man is born again, he cannot see the kingdom of God. This is a core spiritual truth of the Christian faith laid down by Christ in person. Yet in John 3:4, we see Nicodemus confusing this new birth experience with a physical birth. In John 3:4, Nicodemus asked how a man can be born when he is old, considering that surely he cannot enter a second time into his mother's womb to be born. Nicodemus, a leader of Israel, failed to grasp the truth of Christ's teaching and so he asked the question in order to better understand.

It is alright to ask questions. The Bible commends the Bereans in Acts 17:11 with being of more noble character than the Thessalonians because they received the Word with great eagerness and examined the Scriptures every day to determine whether Paul spoke the truth. If you are sincerely searching for the truth, God will answer your questions. A good way to know false doctrines is to know the true teachings of our Lord and Savior Jesus Christ. Jesus Christ sent a teacher to those that believe in Him. The name of this teacher is the Holy Spirit. The Holy Spirit can never make a mistake. He is a teacher of truth. To be delivered from false teachings, you must have the right teacher, the Holy Spirit.

Briefly, let us examine the promise of Jesus in John 14:15–17:

> [15] If you love me, you will obey what I command.
> [16] And I will ask the Father, and he will give you another Counselor to be with you forever—

[17] the Spirit of truth. The world cannot accept him, because it neither sees him nor knows him. But you know him, for he lives with you and will be in you.

In John 14:16, Jesus refers to the Holy Spirit as an eternal Counselor and calls him the Spirit of truth. A counselor is an adviser. This Counselor that Jesus talks about is a Spirit that is the personification of Truth. In John 14:26, Jesus further refers to the Holy Spirit as a teacher:

But the Counselor, the Holy Spirit, whom the Father will send in my name, will teach you all things and will remind you of everything I have said to you.

Jesus makes it clear that the world cannot accept the Holy Spirit, the Teacher of truth and the Spirit of truth, because the world has neither seen him nor known him. When you want spiritual truth to be revealed to you, you must depend on the Teacher of truth, the Holy Spirit, to communicate that truth to you through the Holy Bible. Many have sought to study the Holy Bible without the counsel of the Holy Spirit and have ended up merely reading the Word of God like it were ordinary literature. In John 5:39–40, Jesus speaks to the Jews about the futility of diligently studying the Scriptures apart from Him:

[39] You diligently study the Scriptures because you think that by them you possess eternal life. These are the Scriptures that testify about me,
[40] yet you refuse to come to me to have life.

In other words, it is in Christ through the Holy Spirit that truth is revealed. The Holy Spirit is for us believers. You shall know the truth and the truth shall make you free. This is the foundational key for deliverance from a spirit of error, deliverance from seducing and deceiving spirits, and deliverance from strongholds that have taken captive of the mind. False teachers, false prophets, and false apostles are in tandem with seducing and deceiving spirits. By their teachings, by their fruits, you shall know them.

Now that we have a sense of the character of the Holy Spirit, let us examine the character of our adversary, Satan.

Satan is a deceiver and so he is in the business of spreading and passing false teachings as the true teachings of Christ. The work of Satan is to make a lie look like the truth. Revelation 12:9 refers to Satan in his role as deceiver of the whole world. The world is deceived by Satan into believing a lie as truth. This is why Jesus admonishes his disciples beforehand that the world cannot know or accept the Holy Spirit, the Spirit of truth. The fact is that there is another spirit at work in the world that is contrary to the Holy Spirit. It is that other spirit that promotes false teachings in the body of Christ.

In John 8, Jesus, in his lengthy conversation with the Jews, had this to say in verse 44:

"You belong to your father, the devil, and you want to carry out your father's desire. He was a murderer from the beginning, not holding to the truth, for there is no truth in him. When he lies, he speaks his native language, for he is a liar and the father of lies."

In 2 Corinthians 4:4, Paul in his writings to the church in Corinth referred to Satan's work as follows:

"The god of this age has blinded the minds of unbelievers, so that they cannot see the light of the gospel of the glory of Christ, who is the image of God."

Satan has employed various mechanisms of deception to pass a lie as truth. Many are deceived and do not even know they are being deceived on a daily basis. This is because they have not searched the Scriptures like the Bereans did in Acts 17 and they have not asked the Holy Spirit for help. Satan thrives in deception mainly by ensuring that his victims remain ignorant. Ignorance is a platform for deception. Knowledge, wisdom, and understanding carry the power of liberation and deliverance. That is why Satan and his demonic kingdom fight so hard to ensure that people are ignorant of the truth concerning the teachings of Christ and the acts of the Holy Spirit. In furtherance of his demonic agenda of deception, Satan is adept at transforming himself into an angel of light so that the unsuspecting and the undiscerning do not see him for who he really is. Satan and his demons will sometimes manifest as angels of light in order to deceive the children of light. Unfortunately, some in our churches are being led by a familiar spirit, and they are convinced they are being led by the Holy Spirit. Believers, wake up! The devil is a liar.

The Apostle Paul gives us a pertinent warning in 2 Corinthians 11:13–15:

13 For such men are false apostles, deceitful workmen, masquerading as apostles of Christ.

14 And no wonder, for Satan himself masquerades as an angel of light.

15 It is not surprising, then, if his servants masquerade as servants of righteousness. Their end will be what their actions deserve.

Do you want to be delivered from false teachings and false prophecies? Do not be easily moved by signs and wonders. Be moved by character. Jesus says that by their fruits you shall know them. Practitioners of darkness also perform miracles. This is why we must be discerning in order to avoid sitting under a false teaching.

In Matthew 24, Jesus warns believers about the coming of false Christs, false teachers, and false prophets. False teachers are particularly very dangerous because they have the ability, and sometimes the audience, to spread false teachings and doctrines rapidly.

Once you know the truth, it will begin to work out your deliverance. Yes, you shall know the truth and the truth shall make you free. You can be anointed, sanctified, and speaking in tongues, but in the area where you are lacking in knowledge, you are liable to be deceived. In Hosea 4:6 we see that the people of God are destroyed by lack of knowledge. Do not allow yourself to be destroyed by a lack of knowledge. Begin to know the truth. It is the truth that sets you free from Satan's lies.

The Bible admonishes us in 2 Corinthians 13:5 to examine ourselves to see whether we are in the faith. In 1 Corinthians 10:12 we are cautioned that if we think we are standing firm, we must be careful lest we fall. In effect, being delivered from false teachings requires our willingness to cooperate with the Spirit of truth that will put us through a test to show us where we stand.

There are some false teachings that have crept into the body of Christ. When these teachings are examined in light of Scripture, there is no biblical basis for upholding them. In many believers, some of these teachings have become strongholds. To secure release from bondage, a lie must be seen as a lie. This certainly requires an encounter with truth. Strongholds induced by false teachings and demonic involvement begin to be demolished as the truth of the gospel of Jesus Christ is consistently applied through obedience to Christ's teachings.

2 Corinthians 10:3–5:

> ³ For though we live in the world, we do not wage war as the world does.

[4] The weapons we fight with are not the weapons of the world. On the contrary, they have divine power to demolish strongholds.

[5] We demolish arguments and every pretension that sets itself up against the knowledge of God, and we take captive every thought to make it obedient to Christ.

Many Christians battle with strongholds in their minds and spirits that enslave and hinder them from receiving the truth of God's Word. In his book *Healing the Nations*, John Loren Sandford defines a mental stronghold as "a practiced way of thinking that has become ingrained and automatic. It has a life and a will of its own. Strongholds are areas of the mind in which we are held captive and perceptions are distorted." Only the truth of God's Word can deliver us from these strongholds and false teachings. The truth of the Word demands our repentance and obedience. Those that are fond of making excuses are not ready for their deliverance and are comfortable being where they are. For deliverance you must be desperate like blind Bartimaeus and cry out to Christ that you might see. You cannot see in darkness. It is the light that will reveal the darkness. The light shines in the darkness, and the darkness cannot withstand or comprehend it.

Let us begin to review and examine a few false teachings that have crept into modern-day Christianity. If you believe these teachings to be true, please still take the pains to examine them in light of Scripture. In fact, the Bible implores you to examine yourself and your beliefs. Engaging in an exercise of self-examination is quite biblical and is actually a demonstration of humility. The prideful think they know it all and so are unwilling to go through a process of self-examination. Remember, the platform for deception is rooted in our ignorance. The cure for ignorance is true knowledge and understanding. The sole custodian of truth is our Lord Jesus Christ, who has given us believers the Spirit of truth.

One subtle way that false teachers introduce false teachings into the church is by teaching one biblical truth to the exclusion of others. Paul enjoins Timothy to rightly divide the word of truth. When the word of truth is rightly divided, a dangerous imbalance is avoided. We are now in the era where the church is struggling to endure sound doctrine. Apostle Paul warns about this in 2 Timothy 4:3–4:

> For the time will come when men will not put up with sound doctrine. Instead, to suit their own desires, they will gather around them a great number of teachers to say what their itching ears want to hear. They will turn their ears away from the truth and turn aside to myths.

The Prosperity Gospel

The prosperity gospel emphasizes carnal prosperity over righteousness and holy living. To a number of leaders in the Christian faith, preaching the gospel has become a business. They have transformed the gospel of the cross into a "name it and claim it" gospel—to their followers, their message is primarily about sowing seeds to reap a harvest. Jesus never commanded that money be put down to receive a miracle. Most times, Jesus demanded having faith as a prerequisite to receiving a miracle. Let us assume that a mustard seed is the smallest denomination of currency. In Luke 17:6, when Jesus talks about faith as a mustard seed, he is not saying that faith is such a seed—he is saying that it can be likened to a mustard seed. Giving is very important. However, your giving must not be manipulated or influenced by the desire to receive. If it is, then you are attempting to purchase a miracle. I have received many miracles from Christ, and they have all been received by faith. While sowing is important, it must be emphasized that this is not the gospel's central theme. Its central theme is the death, burial, and resurrection of our Lord Jesus Christ *(1 Cor. 15:4)*. This calls for living a sacrificial life and not a life of greed coupled with carnal ease. John 16:33 tells us that in this world we will have trouble. Acts 14:22 tells us that we must go through many tribulations to enter the kingdom of heaven.

Undoubtedly, there is a nexus between sowing and reaping. It is true that your giving is tied to your receiving. This is true but is not an embodiment of the whole truth on the matter. It is true in the sense that it is a part of the truth. The idea that we could just sow a few dollar seeds or hundreds of dollars in seed money, without seeking God, is absurd. Hebrews 11:6, in part, tells us that God is a rewarder of those who diligently seek Him. Before you sow that seed make sure you have diligently sought God. Otherwise, you may be wasting your seed.

Indeed it is true that the will of God is that we prosper as believers. Yet, by the rightly dividing of Scripture, we cannot fail to realize that Christ spoke against storing up treasures on earth in Matthew 6:19–24. The reason for Jesus's coming was not to give man gold and silver. He came to save man from sin. Little wonder no one, except Jesus, regarded the poor widow's two mites in Luke 21. More important than the amount you give is the condition of your heart. Have you succumbed to the false teaching that encourages you to seek riches and pray for riches and yet you have failed to examine your life to see if you are bearing the fruit of the Spirit? Do you serve God for money or for eternal life? Jesus makes it clear that it is impossible to serve two masters *(Matt. 6:24)*. It's either you serve Mammon (the god of money) or you serve God. Matthew 6:33 enjoins us to seek first the kingdom of God and His righteousness and that all other things will be added unto us. Furthermore, in the parable of the sower in Mark 4:19, Christ speaks about the deceitfulness of riches. We must be very careful. Money is very important, but we must not elevate it to the status of becoming a god in our lives. Abraham was a wealthy man, and he was willing to give up his wealth, even his Isaac, unto the Lord God. This is in contrast with the rich young ruler in the time of Christ that walked away sad because the thought of giving up his wealth to follow Christ was unimaginable. How many wealthy bishops, apostles, pastors, evangelists, and believers can pass the test that the rich young ruler failed? Christ wants to be your number one priority. He does not want the carnal desire for riches competing with him for first place in your life.

Even before the birth of Christ, the get-rich-quick syndrome has been a problem. In Joshua 7, we see Achan stealing treasure from the enemy's camp in total disregard of the Lord's covenant. The consequence: death. Why? Because the prosperity gospel is founded in carnality.

Romans 8:5–8 states:

> 5 Those who live according to the sinful nature have their minds set on what that nature desires; but those who live in accordance with the Spirit have their minds set on what the Spirit desires.
>
> 6 The mind of sinful man is death, but the mind controlled by the Spirit is life and peace;
>
> 7 The sinful mind is hostile to God. It does not submit to God's law, nor can it do so.
>
> 8 Those controlled by the sinful nature cannot please God.

What controls the desire to have more and more and yet not be satisfied? The flesh. This prosperity gospel that over-emphasizes prosperity is pampered by the flesh, the carnal desire of man that is at variance with God. The Bible says that it "shall be added unto you." You do not have to engage in manipulation and arm twisting to obtain riches. Promotion and riches come from the Lord. It is for this reason that Paul perhaps charges Timothy in 1 Timothy 6:9–11 thus:

[9] People who want to get rich fall into temptation and a trap and into many foolish and harmful desires that plunge men into ruin and destruction.

[10] For the love of money is a root of all kinds of evil. Some people, eager for money, have wandered from the faith and pierced themselves with many griefs.

[11] But you, man of God, flee from all this, and pursue righteousness, godliness, faith, love, endurance and gentleness.

The Demonization of Christians

Another false teaching that has deprived many in the body of Christ of deliverance is that once one becomes a Christian, he or she cannot have demons. This teaching ignores occurrences in the Bible and fails to examine the lives of believers who are experiencing mild to severe forms of demonic invasions in their body and soul. I have yet to find a Scripture that says it is impossible for a believer to be demonized. On the other hand, there are some Scriptures showing the demonization of believers in the gospels and the book of Acts. The Bible shows us that there is a spirit of infirmity.

In Luke 13, we come across a woman who Christ called the daughter of Abraham. In John 8:37–44, Jesus lets the Jews know that they cannot claim Abraham as their father unless they were doing the things that Abraham did. He tells them plainly that the devil is their father. In the mind of Christ, a child of Abraham is a child in obedience and relationship with God. With this understanding, we know that the woman of Luke 13 that Christ called a daughter of Abraham was a believer. Romans 4:16 refers to Abraham as the father of all who believe.

In Luke 13:10–13, we see Jesus heal a crippled woman on the Sabbath. This passage is very critical to our understanding of whether a believer can have a demon working inside of him or her:

¹⁰ On a Sabbath Jesus was teaching in one of the synagogues,

¹¹ and a woman was there who had been crippled by a spirit of infirmity for eighteen years. She was bent over and could not straighten up at all.

¹² When Jesus saw her, he called her forward and said to her, "Woman, you are set free from your infirmity."

¹³ Then he put his hands on her, and immediately she straightened up and praised God.

In Luke 13:11, we see that the woman's crippled condition was caused by a spirit of infirmity. A spirit of infirmity is a demon:

Many were indignant because Jesus set her free from the demon of infirmity on the Sabbath day.

In Luke 13:16, Jesus responds thus:

"Then should not this woman, a daughter of Abraham, whom Satan has kept bound for eighteen long years, be set free on the Sabbath day from what bound her?"

Jesus's reference to this woman as a daughter of Abraham shows that she was a believer and yet she had a spirit of infirmity, a demon, operating within her and causing her to be crippled.

For years, many Christians have been taught that a demon cannot co-dwell in the same body as the Holy Spirit. This teaching may sound logical and reasonable, but it is not scriptural. You see, the natural man cannot understand the things of the spirit because they are spiritually discerned. The natural man uses his five senses to draw conclusions regardless of what is going on in the realm of the spirit. As a matter of fact, Satan and his demons work very hard to oppose born-again believers and will seek any opening to infiltrate them.

In deliverance ministry, we have come against many demons residing in born-again, tongue-speaking believers. One being saved and baptized in the Holy Spirit is no indication that there is no demonic presence in that person's life. In Luke 10:19 and Mark 16:17, Jesus gives believers the authority to cast out demons. Believers who walk in the flesh instead of in the Spirit are particularly at risk for inviting demonic presence and activity into their lives. The false teaching that claims believers cannot have demons has made many blindly accept all medical diagnoses, prognoses, forms of treatment, and medications. Worse still, this false teaching strengthens demons' resolve to stay in the life of the believer since believers are taught to think that demons cannot be in them.

In the Old Testament, we see the story of a believer whom God commends as His servant. This is the testimony of Job as given by God Almighty in Job 1:8:

> Then the Lord said to Satan, "Have you considered my servant Job? There is no one on earth like him; he is blameless and upright, a man who fears God and shuns evil."

As the events unfold in Job 1 and 2, we see Satan inflict disease and torment upon Job. Job was tormented by a satanic onslaught, and that is not to say that Job had a demon. This only shows how close the enemy can get in the life of a believer.

In Galatians 3:1, Paul asked who had bewitched the believers in Galatia so as to carry them away from the truth. Bewitchment here suggests the workings of evil spirits imposing and enforcing false doctrines upon the Galatian believers through the use of false teachers. The body of Christ must awaken to the truth that demons attack believers. This is why God gave us His whole armor with accompanying mighty weapons of warfare.

Once Saved, Always Saved

The Bible is quite clear about the security of our salvation as believers, and so the question is not whether a believer can lose his salvation. What is at issue is the false teaching that you can say a simple sinner's prayer, confess to Christ as your Savior, and then live your life as you please. The idea that you can wallow in sin and still enter into heaven is false. Do not be deceived by lying spirits that seduce many believers into thinking that their continuously living a life of sin is without eternal consequences. Many think they are going to heaven because they have bribed God with a sinner's prayer, but in fact, they are hell bound! False teaching! Pastors and teachers of the Word, we must warn the people about sin. The wages of sin is death!

We are in the era where many believers don't fear God. The teaching that salvation without responsibility and without good works is sufficient is a teaching from hell. We are not saved by good works. We are saved to do good works. It is your fruit that evidences your salvation and not a sinner's prayer by itself. Many have come to church altars when a call to be born again was given and have said such sinner's prayers, yet the fruit of their lives show that they are not that new creation in Christ. The old things have not passed away to give way to the new man. In salvation there must be genuine repentance and faith working together.

An abuse of grace has been encouraged by a false lackadaisical teaching that emphasizes you can live life as you please and go to heaven. The truth is that the grace of Christ demands repentance and holiness. Every other grace is cheap and often provides a license to sin.

The devil wants you to believe that you can live however you please and that the blood of Jesus will shield you from his attacks. This is a major deception of Satan. The blood of Jesus cannot deliver and protect you if you dine with Satan. One of the ultimate deceptions is to have a form of godliness (mere religiosity) and deny the power thereof. No one is exempt from being susceptible to deception. You could be very religious, going to church every Sunday, and yet be deceived. Satan, by the way, does not respect your religion. Satan and his demons only retreat when they see the power of God demonstrated in your life and you confront them with that power in Jesus' name.

Seducing spirits have taught alternative forms of grace and distorted biblical grace in order to produce lukewarm Christians. These seducing spirits cleverly omit the truth that God will still hold them accountable for their actions. The Apostle Jude writes to believers and reminds them concerning the grace of God in Jude 4:

> For certain men whose condemnation was written about long ago have secretly slipped in among you. They are godless men, who change the grace of our God into a license for immorality and deny Jesus Christ our only Sovereign and Lord.

False teaching that appears to be true is quick to overemphasize Scriptures such as we are saved by grace and not by works *(Eph. 2:8–9)*; that we are no longer sinners but saints in the sight of God *(1 Cor. 1:2)*; and that God's love for us believers is not based on our performance or acts of righteousness *(Rom. 5:6–10)*. While this is so true, the deception lies in the fact that they fail to mention other scriptural warnings about living a life of sin. The Word of truth must be rightly handled and divided in order not to reach unsound conclusions that distort the true intentions of the gospel. Do not fall for any teaching that promotes a license for sinning and thus hinders the Holy Spirit from even convicting you of sin anymore. The Holy Spirit is grieved when believers choose to fall under the deception of such a false teaching. The Holy Spirit is still warning us today about falling prey to false doctrines.

1 Timothy 4:1 states, "The Spirit clearly says that in later times some will abandon the faith and follow deceiving spirits and things taught by demons." The ultimate purpose of false teaching is to get its adherents to abandon the faith.

Many lying and seducing spirits have gone into the world with their demonic agenda of deception and spreading false teachings. We must live free of the corrupting influences of these teachings. We must be delivered from these teachings that produce strongholds in our minds and thus cause us to act in a manner inconsistent with God's Word. The Bible warns us in Matthew 24 of the appearance of false Christs. Just as there are false Christs, there are false gospels, false apostles, false prophets, false pastors, false teachers, and false ministers. Satan is fond of raising up false teachers to spread false doctrines and thus, deceive men to eternal damnation.

Indeed, by their fruit you will know them. False ministers produce false signs and wonders—signs and wonders that are not verifiable and cannot endure under the scrutiny of light. Beware of Satan's false teachings and practices because there are so many counterfeits that look like the real thing but their source is not God.

To further his deception, the devil will sow tares (evil ones) among the wheat (sons of God). The tares resemble wheat, but they are counterfeit. It is these tares in positions of leadership and authority that begin to teach such falsehoods like: (i) the gifts of the Holy Spirit are no longer in operation, (ii) Christians cannot have demons, (iii) you can live a life of evil, practice evil, and yet be saved and heaven bound. Take heed, you shall reap what you sow! Repent! (iv) there is no hell, etc. Satan has released a multitude of lying spirits to twist the Scriptures and pave way for the coming of the antichrist and new world order with one world religion and one world government.

There is an urgency now, more than ever before, to study, know, and apply the Word of God. All false doctrines are, of course, evil doctrines and open the door for evil spirits to operate in the lives of those who embrace these doctrines. Hence, the need for discernment. If you lack discernment, you are susceptible to fall prey to Satan's deception. Satan uses questionable divine revelations and adulterated teachings to deceive. We must guard against New Age philosophies creeping into our churches and our lives.

Further, we must develop a deep hunger for God's Word. God will not work against His Word. God has exalted His Word above His name *(Ps. 138:2)*. It is in your interest to begin to judge all things according to 1 Corinthians 2:15. Investigate and examine the things and practices you are walking in through the Word of God. For example, if you investigate and examine the Scriptures, you will discover that the blood of Jesus cannot cover you effectively if you are giving ground to Satan. You cannot serve Satan and plead the blood of Jesus at the same time. It won't work because that is engaging in hypocrisy. The blood of Jesus is activated by your obedience *(Exod. 12, 13)*.

To get deliverance in this area, as a Christian you must begin to study and meditate upon the Word of God with the guidance of your Counselor, the Holy Spirit. You must begin to fervently pray for discernment and learn how to try the spirits. 1 John 4:1 tells us not to believe every spirit but rather to test the spirits to determine whether they are from God, because many false prophets have gone out into the world.

We know that we are children of God, and that the whole world is under the control of the evil one *(1 John 5:19)*.

Satan is a master deceiver who works tirelessly to deceive you, me, and all of humanity. He also works to deceive nations and global powers such as the United Nations, World Bank, huge multinational corporations, and conglomerates.

To be delivered from deception and false doctrines, you must denounce all pride and examine your ways and lifestyle to ensure the devil has not gained an advantage over you. The key is to always grow and abound in discernment. Without spiritual eyes, you can be in the midst of a mighty act of God and not recognize it. Those who are spiritually dead cannot see or understand spiritual things. Spiritual sensitivity to God is a quality that must be developed and exercised in order to stay free of false teachings and deception. If you are not discerning, you will not be able to tell the real from the fake and the fake from the real. This was the case when God visited his people in the person of his Son, but many did not recognize him when he came *(John 1:10–12)*.

Prayers of Deliverance from Seducing Spirits

Meditate upon the following Scriptures: 2 Corinthians 11:13–15; 1 Timothy 4:1–2; and Revelation 2:20–25. Pray as follows:

1. In the name of Jesus, let the light of God expose any false teaching that I have held on to as truth.
2. In the name of Jesus, I reject and renounce every teaching that does not align with the Word of God.
3. In the name of Jesus, I pull down every vain imagination and contrary thought induced by false teachings of the prosperity gospel and embrace holiness as my priority in Jesus' name.
4. I bind every seducing spirit responsible for presenting me with false teachings in the name of Jesus and ask that the blood of Jesus cleanse me from all defilements thereof.
5. In the name of Jesus, I ask for a spirit of discernment to know the true from the false.

6. Lord, I repent for allowing the spirit of Jezebel to teach me Your Word and pull down every stronghold Jezebel planted in my mind in the name of Jesus Christ.

2

THE YOKE OF ENTANGLEMENT

Brother January came off the streets of New York City to our ministry, Overcomers in Christ Faith Assembly, in 2014. Brother January was homeless and bound by addictions and unforgiveness. He confessed and professed Christ but was heavily populated with demons. It was difficult to get him to keep still in our meetings. Demonic manifestations within him were quite frequent and intense. Quickly, with the help of the Holy Spirit, we began binding and casting out demonic strongmen and beings that claimed ownership of him. We rejected their assertions of ownership and influence and insisted on enforcing God's Word in Brother January's life.

We knew we had to work on disentangling Brother January from longstanding curses and demonic strongholds that had taken firm root in his mind. As he began the process of deliverance, we saw undeniable changes in his demeanor and character. His true identity in Christ, which had been suppressed by demonic powers, started to emerge. The spirits of addiction proved to be very stubborn though. Over the course of a few months, we succeeded in casting out these evil spirits. By the following week, Brother January was free of cravings for nicotine and alcohol.

Now, with the influence of addiction behind him, it became easier to minister the Word of God to Brother January. Through the Word of God, he began to see that he is a new creation in Christ Jesus. Continuing with Brother January's deliverance, the Holy Spirit pointed us to the presence of evil spirits of infirmity and death. We immediately fought with these demons. They would manifest and yet refuse to be cast out. Eventually these spirits were forcibly removed from Brother January in the name of Jesus.

Over the course of time, because we were dealing with legions of demons, we had to keep those inside of him bound in the name of Jesus until we were ready to fight them again and cast them out. In Jesus' name, we kept many of these demons bound and rendered them powerless in Brother January's life. Today, we have no doubt that he is on the road to complete freedom. He is clean and tidy in appearance. The yoke of entanglement that the kingdom of darkness put on him was addiction. Once that yoke was broken, it became less difficult to deal with the underlying persona of darkness that kept him chained to a life of hopelessness.

Just like Brother January, many in the body of Christ are struggling with some form of addiction. Addiction is a strong, persistent, and compulsive habit of dependency on a dangerous activity such as substance abuse, gambling, sex, and so forth. Many believers are laboring under an unrelenting yoke of entanglement and are in desperate need of deliverance from it.

Entanglement hinders you from doing what you have been called to do. Entanglements will keep you from going to places that you have been called to go and from being what you have been called to be. Entanglement hinders personal and spiritual development. If you do not grow, you will decay.

Satan uses entanglements to stifle the believer's mission for Christ. Apostle Paul in 2 Timothy 2:4 (KJV) tells Timothy that:

"No man that warreth entangleth himself with the affairs of this life; that he may please him who hath chosen him to be a soldier."

As a believer, you are at war with forces of darkness. Ephesians 6:12 tells us that we wrestle not against flesh and blood, but against principalities, powers, rulers of the darkness of this world, and spiritual wickedness in high places. In a war, to maintain your advantage over the enemy you must avoid entanglements. The enemy wants you entangled so that he can have dominion over you. You must do all within your means not to be entangled so that you are free to be what you have been called by God to be. Proverbs 6:5 advises:

Free yourself, like a gazelle from the hand of the hunter, like a bird from the snare of the fowler.

When a gazelle is entangled in a trap, it desperately does all it can to come out of that trap. A goat, on the other hand, is different. It may be caught in a trap and would not mind so long as there is grass for it to eat in that trap. The gazelle is not looking for food when freedom is at stake. Do not be a believer who is content with being entangled so long as he is given grass to eat by the enemy. This may sound ludicrous but there are many believers entangled in the snare of a welfare system that encourages poverty. They are content to stay in the snare because they are fed grass within the snare. Be like the gazelle. Do not be like the goat. Begin to disentangle yourself. If need be, go for deliverance just like Brother January did.

Stand fast therefore in the liberty wherewith Christ hath made us free and be not entangled again with the yoke of bondage *(Gal. 5:1, KJV)*.

Christ came to set us free from the yoke of bondage that entangled us. Galatians 5:1 describes entanglement as being a yoke of bondage. As we begin to examine the various devices of entanglement that Satan uses to keep believers bound, we begin to appreciate the urgency in putting to destruction every chain of entanglement restraining us from realizing the fullness of our potential. Hebrews 12:1 admonishes us to throw off everything that hinders and the sin that so easily entangles so that we may run with perseverance the race marked out for us. One notable point: Everything that hinders is an entanglement. In addition, sin easily entangles us.

Sin

Hebrews 12:1 talks about casting away sin because it easily entangles us and draws us back from running our race with perseverance. Concerning sin, it has been rightly said that sin does three things to believers:

1. Sin will always take you farther than you intended to go.
2. Sin will always keep you longer than you are willing to stay.
3. Sin will always cost you more than you thought it would.

From the above, we can see the entangling, crippling power of sin. In Romans 8:2, we see that sin is a law. This means that it remains in operation until it is revoked. It is the law of the Spirit of life in Christ Jesus that sets us free from the law of sin. It is only the law of Christ that can revoke, annul, and forbid the law of sin from being in operation in our lives. It is futile attempting to modify or amend the law of sin. The law of sin must be revoked, and only the law of the Spirit of life in Christ Jesus has the power to do so. When the law of sin is revoked in our lives, we are set free from sin, which easily entangles.

Therefore, there is now no condemnation for those who are in Christ Jesus, because through Christ Jesus the law of the Spirit of life set me free from the law of sin and death. For what the law was powerless to do in that it was weakened by the sinful nature, God did by sending his own Son in the likeness of sinful man to be a sin offering. And so he condemned sin in sinful man, in order that the righteous requirements of the law might be fully met in us, who do not live according to the sinful nature but according to the Spirit *(Rom. 8:1–3).*

Sin is a law that entangles, and the law of Christ sets us free from this entangling law. We must be delivered from the entanglement of sin through the power of Jesus Christ.

In the book of Judges, we see Samson, who was chosen by God to lead His people out of Philistinian bondage. God equipped Samson with the strength needed to fulfill his task. However, Samson consistently lived a reckless life of sin that literally caused him to be entangled by an agent of his enemies. Samson often entertained the occasion for sinning and ended up progressing from one level of bondage to a higher level until he eventually lost his vision and suffered imprisonment at the hands of his enemies.

Addiction

One of the major problems facing the United States today is drug addiction. It has grown so severe that America is spending billions of dollars fighting a war on drugs. The drug culture is prevalent in the school system, the prison system, the workplace, and on the streets. It has permeated American society to such a degree that the United States remains the largest consumer of illegal drugs in the world. Drugs create an irresistible dependency on the user. Drug abuse has caused so much damage in families and in our societies. Satan is pleased when man is addicted to a hard substance because addiction provides an easy mechanism for demonic control. Addictions tend to start off as a coping mechanism for stress induced by rejection, trauma, and oppression. There is always an underlying reason that feeds an addiction. That reason must seriously be addressed and confronted by the power of God.

An evil spirit is at work behind every type of addiction. That evil spirit's function is to ensure that the victim is in a helpless self-destructive state. The demon keeps the victim bound to a destructive habit. When that demon of addiction is bound and cast out, we begin to notice immediate changes. Now, there are different types of demons responsible for various forms of addictive behavior.

Addiction comes in the forms of substance abuse, alcohol dependency, gambling, gluttony, painkillers, sex—especially masturbation—and much more. The spirit of addiction works behind the scenes to produce a compulsive desire and craving to engage in destructive addictive habits.

If you are ensnared by an addiction and have been in many programs with little success, now is the time to come to Jesus Christ. The Bible says in John 8:36 that if Christ sets you free you will truly be free. This means you will no longer be bound and drained by a spirit of addiction. Christ desires to set all who are willing free from the use of cigarettes, alcohol, and drugs.

> For you did not receive a spirit that makes you a slave again to fear, but you received the Spirit of sonship. And by him we cry *"Abba,* Father." The Spirit himself testifies with our spirit that we are God's children *(Rom. 8:15–16).*

Romans 8:15–16 mentions three kinds of spirits in the realm of the spirit. The spirit that makes one a slave again to fear is the spirit of bondage. This particular evil spirit that enslaves people through addiction and other means must be bound and cast out in Jesus' name. The second spirit is the Spirit of sonship, otherwise called the Spirit of adoption. This is a ministering spirit that is from God and of God. This Spirit must be loosed to destroy all demonic entanglements of addiction and to usher us into sonship with the One we call *Abba*, Father. The third spirit mentioned in this passage is our own spirit—the spirit of man. It is the spirit of man that must cry out for deliverance and pray that the spirit of sonship dominates and drives out the spirit responsible for putting man in bondage. A victim of addiction must be determined to be free. He must be disgusted by his addictive habit and the factors that drive the addiction. You cannot love your addiction and seek deliverance from it at the same time. The more one feeds an addiction, the more entangled he becomes by it.

Relationships

Another yoke of entanglement that many believers need deliverance from is the yoke of toxic relationships. This is not limited to evil relationships and associations. There are some relationships that are not evil per se but yet are not profitable. Hebrews 12:1 views those kind of good relationships not as the sin that easily entangles but as the weight that hinders.

> Be ye not unequally yoked together with unbelievers: for what fellowship hath righteousness with unrighteousness? And what communion hath light with darkness? *(2 Cor. 6:14, KJV)*.

The above injunction in 2 Corinthians is not limited to marriage as some suppose. It applies also to business, ministry, and close personal relationships. The kingdom of darkness likes to get believers entangled with unbelievers in order to derail them from their divine destinies. In seeking deliverance from entanglements in evil relationships, we must renounce and cut off every link with such relationship. There may be a price to pay for breaking away from them, but nonetheless, be like that gazelle in the book of Proverbs that does everything to be free from the trap of the hunter.

Deliverance from evil relationships will require the breaking of soul ties. Some believers' problems are that they are entangled by ungodly soul ties. The soul houses the emotions, the mind, and the intellect of man. When one's emotions are constantly and severely influenced by the behavior of another, a soul tie may exist between them. In other words, your closeness to a person in the past may create a soul tie that entangles you and hinders you from moving forward. Such closeness may be sexual or nonsexual. For instance, an ungodly soul tie comes into focus when a man and a woman have sex outside of marriage or when members of the same sex engage in sexual acts with one another. When this soul tie is in operation, it makes it difficult for one of the parties to transition into a meaningful godly relationship because ties of the past are influencing the present.

The soul ties of the past must be broken and renounced in the name of Jesus. For instance, there are women who have said they will never have anything to do with a man because men have hurt them emotionally. Remember, our emotions are housed in the soul. Men also have made these types of assertions about women, because they have been hurt emotionally by women. In this scenario, the problem is that an ungodly soul tie connected to their past is keeping them entangled in the past. Until they are delivered from the harmful effects of this ungodly soul tie planted in their mind and emotions, they will often experience hindrances in future relationships.

In the name of Jesus Christ, you must begin to command all demons associated with soul ties formed through unholy sexual relations out of your life.

Deuteronomy 22:10 warns against being entangled in relationships not pleasing to God. In metaphoric language, we are instructed not to plow with an ox and an ass yoked together. There is a reason for this command. The ox generally is a hardworking animal. The ox desires to work and bring in the harvest. The ass on the other hand is lazy. The ass longs to play, take it easy, and not sweat. The ass is not ready to make sacrifices. And so as time progresses, the ass begins to frustrate the ox when yoked together. So long as that ox is yoked with an ass, it cannot reach the fullness of its potential. What has happened here is that the enemy has yoked this ox with an ass in order to have access into the life of the ox. Now the enemy can start using the ass to torment and frustrate the ox. The ox becomes unhappy and discouraged as a result of its being unequally yoked with a stranger. This is what the devil has done in the lives of many believers. Many believers find themselves in bondage by what they have been yoked with. They are seeking deliverance but are not sure how to go about it.

> What harmony is there between Christ and Belial? What does a believer have in common with an unbeliever? What agreement is there between the temple of God and idols? . . . Therefore come out from them and be separate, says the Lord. Touch no unclean thing and I will receive you *(2 Cor. 6: 15–17).*

There is no harmony between the ox and the ass. Satan thrives in disharmony and discord. The solution is to break the yoke that holds the ox bound to the ass. In marriage, this is not to be seen as encouraging divorce. In certain marriages, however, a form of separation may be necessary for the righteous party to receive deliverance from the entanglements caused by being in an unequally yoked relationship.

Employment

For some believers, the devil has used their employment (a blessing) to entangle them in a manner that hinders them from doing what God requires of them.

In Matthew 4:18–20, we read how Peter and Andrew immediately dropped their nets to follow Jesus. Bear in mind that their nets represented their means of livelihood. Nets are used to catch fish, catch animals, and to catch men on the run. This account in Matthew 4 tells us that Peter and Andrew dropped their nets to follow Jesus wholeheartedly. The dropping of their nets, which represented the essence of their employment as fishermen, showed that they would not permit their vocation to stand in the way of their calling by Christ. Dropping their nets ensured they would not become entangled. After Christ's resurrection and before his ascension, he appeared to Simon Peter in John 21. Peter had picked up his net again! Christ appears to Peter and questions Peter concerning Peter's love for him. Christ makes Peter understand that he must feed and take care of Christ's sheep to demonstrate his love for Christ. And then one more time, Jesus instructs Peter to follow him *(John 21:19)*.

Some believers are so entangled by their jobs that they wind up working extremely long hours seven days a week. They are entangled by what was initially designed to be a blessing and are prevented from following Jesus wholeheartedly. Their job is now preventing their spiritual development. If care is not taken, Satan and his cohorts of demons will begin to use that job that God blessed that believer with to cause the believer to backslide. What a tragedy it is for a blessing to be converted into a curse simply because the believer was entangled and wrapped up in that blessing instead of holding fast to Jesus Christ, the One that is the Jehovah Jireh.

Debt

Another yoke of entanglement in Satan's armory is the yoke of debt. This yoke is designed to tempt man to live a life above his means by mortgaging his future to pay for his present cravings. Ultimately, the yoke of debt coupled with unbearable interest rates entangle man in poverty. Even governments are not free from the burden and yoke of debt. Central banks, including the Federal Reserve Banks, often reduce interest rates to encourage people to borrow more. Over-dependency on the extension of credit becomes a snare, and in some cases, an addiction that many must be delivered from. A key blessing mentioned in Deuteronomy 28:12 is that if we are obedient, the Lord will open the heavens, the storehouse of his bounty, to send rain on our land in season and to bless all the work of our hands. We will lend to many nations but will borrow from none. To be a lender is a blessing. To be a borrower may be a curse *(Deut. 28:44)*.

As believers, we must learn to live within our means. We must invest more in the kingdom and less in our appearance and comforts. It is foolishness to use credit to finance the gratification of the flesh. In an attempt to impress others, some believers have taken on debt to finance a luxurious item. Oftentimes, the devil is able to keep many entangled in debt because of their unholy, carnal, and uncontrollable appetites for material things. As a result, many have become financially impotent and unable to go on mission trips or extend other forms of assistance that God may be requiring of them. Worse still, the devil wants believers enslaved by debt so that they have less or nothing to finance the gospel with. In the category of believers who earn very high incomes are those that give a mere pittance for the running of God's house and God's work.

A few times, Christian speakers have held prosperity seminars, preached prosperity messages, and emphasized the principle of sowing and reaping. They have encouraged the people to sow money into the work of the kingdom of God if they want to be blessed. While this is true, we must also emphasize that if you want to prosper financially, while sowing like a farmer in anticipation of the harvest, you must remove the weeds that hinder a bountiful harvest. The weeds that hinder prosperity in our lives include debt, inadequate financial planning, and not understanding the signs of the times. Christian speakers must adopt a more comprehensive approach in teaching principles of prosperity.

Curses

Generally speaking, a curse is an evil pronouncement or an evil oath that is enforced by an evil spirit. A strong man is assigned to ensure that the person under the curse remains under the workings of that curse for the appointed time, which often is a lifetime. A man who is entangled by a curse must seek to break it so that he can be released from its evil influences and opposition. Curses originate from diverse sources in the spirit realm. There are occult incantations, witchcraft and psychic spells, ancestral and generational curses, the curse of the land, the curse of the law, and self-inflicted curses. God may also put someone under a curse. These forms of curses are yokes of oppression and entanglement that must be broken.

Just like in the area of whether Christians can have demons, many Christians have been taught erroneously that a Christian cannot be under a curse. It is important to note that Jesus became a curse that we might receive a blessing. Galatians 3:13–14 states:

> [13] Christ redeemed us from the curse of the law by becoming a curse for us, for it is written: "Cursed is everyone who is hung on a tree."
> [14] He redeemed us in order that the blessing given to Abraham might come to the Gentiles through Christ

Jesus, so that by faith we might receive the promise of the Spirit.

Salvation is the experience of having our sins forgiven and our being born again. As we work out our salvation with fear and trembling *(Phil. 2:12)*, we will need to pursue deliverance from things and beings that hinder the benefits of our full salvation in Christ. One of these things is curses. The fact that your sins are forgiven does not mean that curses from the kingdom of darkness are all broken. Many times, curses are hidden. They are not easily apparent but they can be discerned through their workings and evil patterns. The evil pattern may be that certain oppressive incidents always occur at certain times. Such a curse operates under a time covenant.

In Deuteronomy 28, God asks the Israelites to make a choice between life and blessings on the one hand, and death and curses on the other. God laid out the terms of the blessings and the consequences of the curses. God asked the Israelites to choose. God was not going to choose for them. They had to make the choice. The choice they would make would determine their destinies and that of their descendants.

To disentangle ourselves from curses, we must depend on the leading of the Holy Spirit and hold steadfastly to Christ's blood sacrifice for us on the cross. As a Christian, you cannot be living in sin and rebellion and expect curses working against you to be broken. Rebellion is as the sin of witchcraft. We must repent of all sin and rebellion in order to have God's mercy extended in our favor.

One thing that gives a curse a power of its own over a believer is unforgiveness in the life of that believer. Unforgiven sin and sins covered up in secrecy act as barriers in the breaking of curses. God in Christ Jesus provided for the forgiveness of our sins. We must confess our sins in order to be forgiven of our sins. In 1 John 1:9, the Bible says, "If we confess our sins, he is faithful and just and will forgive us our sins and purify us from all unrighteousness." There are some types of sin that may have opened the door for a curse to be imposed upon a believer. Until the believer confesses and repents of that sin, the curse will have power over him. In Deuteronomy 28, we see that descendants also bear the consequences of the choices their ancestors made. Thus, we must not only confess our sins, we must confess the sins of our ancestors. Ancestral sin has entangled many Christians and they are unaware of the root of their problems. To walk in total liberty, you must ask God to release you from the consequences of your ancestors' sins.

Sister February loves the Lord. She came to our ministry, Overcomers in Christ Faith Assembly, for prayers because according to her, she was having evil dreams and things were just not working out for her. As we began to pray for Sister February, it became apparent that she was in need of deliverance. We had no doubt that she loved the Lord and was a born-again believer. However, as deliverance progressed, demons began to manifest and we found out that Sister February's mother was a witch. Several years later, Sister February was suffering the consequences of her mother's sins. Who is to tell what pledge or commitment Sister February's mother may have made regarding Sister February? Sister February came to us because she needed to work out her salvation with fear and trembling. The Lord led us to take good time in breaking witchcraft curses that were working against her. Now we look at her and see less confusion and an inner assurance of peace in the stead of turmoil.

In working to get disentangled from the yoke of a curse, you must forgive all people who have hurt you or betrayed you or wronged you. If you seek God's forgiveness, then you must be willing to forgive others. The sin of unforgiveness is very costly. It keeps the believer bound and entangled on so many levels and fronts.

We must separate ourselves from and renounce all occult and satanic involvements, including satanic objects and satanic associations. You cannot walk in agreement with Satan and ask God to break satanic curses upon you. To walk and work with God, you must be in absolute agreement with Him *(Amos 3:3)*. As you come into agreement with God, begin to pray fervently and cancel all satanic claims against you and ask the Lord Jesus Christ to release you from every curse upon your life.

Unforgiveness

As mentioned previously, unforgiveness is a major barrier to receiving blessings from God in the spirit realm. Satan and his demons work the flesh, the carnal and fleshly desires of man, to keep man entangled in bitterness, offense, strife, and consequently, unforgiveness. The devil raises up people to offend believers so that believers are hurt and carry the venom of the hurt in their spirits. As believers, we must learn to quickly release that hurt and forgive the one that offended us.

> Then Peter came to Jesus and asked, "Lord, how many times shall I forgive my brother when he sins against me? Up to seven times?"
> Jesus answered, "I tell you, not seven times, but seventy-seven times" *(Matt. 18:21–22)*.

Jesus subsequently tells a parable of a servant whose great debt was forgiven by his master but who refused to forgive a small debt owed him by a fellow servant. As a result, the master handed over the unforgiving servant to the jailers to be tormented. Christ warns that this is how God will treat each one unless they truly forgive others from the heart. This is why it is very dangerous and unwise to harbor unforgiveness. If you do, regardless of whether you are born again, God will hand you over to the tormentors until you repent. Unforgiveness is a heavy yoke that is destroyed simply by a sincere decision to forgive in spite of the hurt. The forgiveness must come from the heart. Forgiveness that is not from the heart is no forgiveness at all. Those that forgive begin to experience a healing from the wounds of their offender and start to experience love in their heart toward the ones that offended them.

Forgiveness is not something that is earned or merited. It is something that is freely given. If we refuse to forgive, we are demonstrating an ingratitude toward God's forgiveness that he extended to us, who are so undeserving. As Christians, we must avoid having an unforgiving heart. An unforgiving spirit will bring God's displeasure and discipline.

Forgiveness is not linked to the size of the offense. Like Jesus was teaching Peter, forgiveness cannot be quantified in terms of the number of times or the magnitude of the sin in need of pardon. What matters is that a person remembers his own forgiveness by God and on that basis, is willing to forgive others.

Fear

It has been consistently emphasized in this chapter that an entanglement is that which hinders one from doing what he has been called to do, going where he has been called to go, being what he has been called to be, and if we might add at this point, receiving what he has been called to receive. Fear is one form of entanglement that the devil uses to paralyze the people of God from moving forward and obtaining their breakthroughs.

In 1 Samuel 17, the Israelites were in battle with the Philistines and had to confront a champion of the Philistines, a giant called Goliath. The entire army of Israel feared confronting Goliath. They were paralyzed by fear at the sight of the obstacle in him. The Philistines raised up Goliath to intimidate Israel. Fear and intimidation work together. Intimidation will make you surrender before your fight even begins. Many Christians are not fighting because they have been encircled by fear and intimidation. They are reluctant to fight for what is rightfully theirs because of fear of backlash from the camp of the enemy. The enemy wants you to give up before the actual fight because he knows that when you fight him in Jesus' name, you will defeat him. So the enemy uses fear and intimidation to discourage and paralyze his victims before a battle is fought. If the devil can get you to succumb to fear and lay down your faith, then he has gotten the upper hand in the fight. Fear and intimidation by Goliath was a mechanism that the Philistines used to control and deceive Israel from fighting them. It took the faith and courage of David to fell and destroy fear and intimidation embodied in the person of Goliath. When you use physical eyes instead of the eyes of faith to look at problems, you can easily be ensnared and entangled by those problems. David did not look at Goliath the way Israel was looking at Goliath. David defeated Goliath.

Among other tricks, the devil uses our past against us. He does this to intimidate us from enjoying the blessings that God has for us in the present and in the future. The devil tells many believers that if they dare do the will of God today, he will broadcast their ugly deeds of the past. The way I got over this threat of Satan was to simply confess and repent of my ugly past. Do not let the spirit of fear entangle you and keep you away from the glorious destiny that God has ordained for you.

Many of us are not where we ought to be because multiple things have entangled us. The Bible states in 1 Corinthians 10:23 that everything is permissible but not everything is beneficial. Everything is permissible but not everything is constructive. The fact that something is lawful and permissible does not necessarily mean that it is beneficial. On a few occasions, people have asked me whether it is sinful for a Christian to drink alcohol. They are quick to point out that Jesus turned water into wine and that Paul encouraged Timothy to drink a little wine for his stomach's sake. The truth is that even though drinking of wine is lawful and permissible, it is not beneficial. It can lead to alcoholic addiction if care is not taken. The devil will try and get us to be entangled by permissible things that are not beneficial, and that is why we will need wisdom to drop our nets.

Prayers to Destroy Yokes of Entanglement

Meditate upon the following Scriptures: Proverbs 6:5; 2 Timothy 2:4; Galatians 5:1; and 2 Corinthians 6:14–17. Pray with faith and power the following prayers:

1. I pray that every yoke of entanglement that I am battling with be destroyed by the reason of the anointing in the name of Jesus. By the power in the blood of Jesus, I command every demonic yoke of entanglement in my life to break now and be destroyed in the name of Jesus.
2. I bind in the name of Jesus every evil spirit assigned to enforce the perpetuation of yokes of entanglement in my life and command these yokes be destroyed by fire in the name of Jesus.
3. In the name of Jesus, I scatter unto destruction every network and series of entanglements created to frustrate me by the conspiracy of darkness.
4. Let every yoke of entanglement and frustration in my life be converted to divine fulfillment in the name of Jesus.
5. Let every satanic burden afflicting me with delays and disappointment be roasted by fire in the name of Jesus.
6. I destroy by the power of the Holy Spirit every yoke of limitation and stagnation upon my life.
7. I command every altar enforcing demonic yokes and burdens upon my life to be destroyed in the name of Jesus. God of Elijah rain down fire upon every altar frustrating my destiny in the mighty name of Jesus.

3

DELIVERANCE FROM DEMONIC DELAYS

When it comes to approaching delays of promises, hopes, and dreams, we must be very discerning. Generally speaking, the approach of many is to simply "wait on the Lord" because "God's time is the best." While this is commendable, the problem with such a simplistic approach is that it does not awaken us to discern what may be causing the delay in the spirit realm. The person may be waiting on God's time, and God's time may have passed. It makes sense to ask God for revelation and guidance concerning stubborn delays that may have kept you in the same spot for a considerable period of time. The source of a particular delay will determine how you handle that delay. Some delays require the waging of violent spiritual warfare because the devil is at work. Other delays may require a time of just waiting on the Lord because the Lord is at work.

There are three sources of delays that work in our lives:

1. God
2. Satan and his demonic network
3. Self-inflicted

When God Delays

Oftentimes, God will delay for a variety of reasons. God will create a delay in the life of one He is interested in when it is clear to Him that if that person receives a particular blessing when he is not prepared to receive it, the blessing will turn out to be unprofitable and a curse. God will delay that person and bring about circumstances that will mature that person to receive the blessing. Many times God will bring a trial into that person's life while delaying the promise so that at the time of fulfillment of the promise, the person is ready.

Satan wants you to get the prize before the appointed time so that you will be confused and ill-equipped to handle it. This is exactly what happened to the prodigal son in Luke 15. The younger son asked for his share of his father's estate before the appointed time. He received his share and squandered it. However, when he came to his senses, after having learned a bitter lesson, God opened the door for him to receive from his father's estate. Later, when he returned home, he was prepared to handle the blessing he could not handle at the time he initially left home. God does not want you to get that desirable thing before the right time and so, out of love for you, He will delay that thing from getting into your hands. Oftentimes the prize will seem within reach, yet out of your grasp. This is so because God wants that thing to remain in your spirit so that you are in prayer concerning it.

In another instance, God may delay a person because the kingdom of darkness has programmed evil to meet that person at a certain place and time. The enemy has a sense of the route you will be taking and when. He will urge you to be in that particular vehicle at a set time because that vehicle has been destined for an accident at that time. God in His infinite mercy will trigger circumstances that will cause you to miss that vehicle. Had God not delayed you, you would have been in that vehicle and faced a fatal accident. At times like these, the delay may not make sense and may cause you to be annoyed, but when you realize the tragedy you escaped because you were delayed, you will thank God for it. God introduces this kind of delay to make sure you are not at the wrong place at the time of danger.

God is in the business of introducing divine delays so that things do not just happen in the natural time when they are expected. God will make things happen in His own timing because He has a plan and purpose in mind.

In 1 Samuel 1:5, we see that the Lord closed Hannah's womb. Hannah's peers were having babies, but Hannah had to wait because God brought a delay into her life by shutting her womb. According to the natural time, Hannah was a woman of childbearing age and ought to have given birth. Hannah experienced a delay because God was working out something. In God's calculation, the baby Hannah was to give birth to, a prophet named Samuel, had to be born at a particular time for a particular task. If he was born too early, Hannah may not have thought of completely dedicating him to the Lord by handing him over to the priest Eli. God needed Samuel to come at the right time so that Eli could train him to a point where God would use him as prophet over the nation of Israel and to anoint two kings. So Hannah had to bear this delay. This delay was not caused by Satan. Satan did not close Hannah's womb. God closed Hannah's womb.

Abraham's wife, Sarah, experienced the same thing in child conception. She did not understand the delay that God was permitting and so she acted in the flesh, according to the law of time and nature, and demanded that her maid, Hagar, give birth to a child for her with Abraham.

God's delay is for our own good, and so we do not need deliverance from it. What we need is the right attitude like Hannah and not so much the attitude of Sarah. Hannah was steadfast in her faith and prayed to God in tears. Sarah, on the other hand, looked for a solution to minimize the delay of a closed womb. This was a solution for which God's counsel was not sought. With God's divine delay, the attitude is to be in fasting and prayer until God moves. In Acts 1:4, the promise of the Spirit was reiterated by Jesus Christ to His disciples:

> On one occasion, while he was eating with them, he gave them this command: "Do not leave Jerusalem, but wait for the gift my Father promised, which you have heard me speak about."

The disciples waited for the manifestation of this promise, earnestly praying in the upper room. When the promise came in Acts 2, it made no announcement. It came as a rushing mighty wind. God may not tell you the exact time, but just wait faithfully. It will surely come to pass.

> For the vision is yet for an appointed time, but at the end it shall speak, and not lie: though it tarry, wait for it; because it will surely come, it will not tarry *(Hab. 2:3, KJV).*

Habakkuk 2:3 is quite revealing. It says even though the vision tarries (delays), it will not tarry (delay). This simply shows us that God's time does not necessarily coincide with our own natural timing and expectations. God gives the Prophet Habakkuk a caveat. He tells him that even if the vision tarries, he should wait for it. God is opening the people's mind to the possibility that there might be a delay. God often uses delay to reveal what is in our hearts and to build up our character. It takes faith to hold on to God's Word when the fulfillment seems so uncertain. Because there is a time difference, we are encouraged to wait for the vision to come.

When God moves, you know it is time to move: He has removed the delay, and the manifestation of the promise is at your doorstep. It was not done by might or by power. It was accomplished by His Spirit.

Self-Inflicted Delay

This is manmade delay, basically caused by the works of the flesh: slothfulness and procrastination. In Genesis 19, God sent angels to destroy Sodom and Gomorrah. God's angels were sent to rescue Lot before the time of destruction. Lot kept lingering, and the destruction was fast approaching. This self-inflicted delay on Lot's part would have caused him his demise. The angels of the Lord had to intervene.

Genesis 19:

> [14] So Lot went out and spoke to his sons-in-law, who were pledged to marry his daughters. He said, "Hurry and get out of this place, because the Lord is about to destroy the city!" But his sons-in-law thought he was joking.
>
> [15] With the coming of dawn, the angels urged Lot, saying, "Hurry, take your wife and your two daughters who are here, or you will be swept away when the city is punished."
>
> [16] When he hesitated, the men grasped his hand and the hands of his wife and of his two daughters and led them safely out of the city, for the Lord was merciful to them.

Had Lot continued wasting time, he would have met an untimely death. Procrastination is dangerous, and without divine help, Lot would have perished with the rest of Sodom. Manmade delay is not profitable and is contrary to God's agenda.

If you are given to slothfulness and procrastination, you have to begin to walk in the Spirit and submit to the leading of the Spirit. Time is very important. You want to be at the right place at the right time—God's time.

Demonic Delays

The delay we really need deliverance from is that caused by powers of darkness. Powers of darkness are located primarily in the heavenly realms and work hard to frustrate us in the earthly realm. Our main focus in this chapter is on demonic delays.

In Daniel 10, Daniel prayed and the prince of Persia delayed the angel sent to him with an answer. It took warfare in the heavenly realms for twenty-one days before the angel could reach Daniel with the answer he sought. There was a twenty-one-day delay caused by a principality of darkness.

How the Spirit of Delay Works

Satan works through a network. Oftentimes the communication a person receives from this deceptive demonic network, if he is not discerning, is that he should keep on waiting because God's time is the best. Before the person knows it, God's true appointed time will pass and his waiting would have been in vain and amounted to nothing. The person is deceived to wait for God to move; meanwhile, God is waiting for the person to move.

Israel experienced a somewhat similar phenomenon in Exodus 14. The Israelites get to the Red Sea with Pharaoh and his army in hot pursuit. In Exodus 14:14, Moses tells the people to be still while he cries out to the Lord. In Exodus 14:15, the Lord asks Moses why he is crying out to him instead of telling the Israelites to move on. If Moses kept still and delayed the crossing of the Red Sea, Pharaoh and his army would have caught up with the Israelites and returned them to captivity in Egypt. It was not the plan of God for Moses and His people to be still at that moment. His plan was for them to move on. Of course, Satan wanted them to wait for Pharaoh to catch up with them. This is what Satan does:

He wants you to be waiting for God when he is executing his attack to rob you of your destiny. That is not the time to wait as Moses learned. It is the time to move on.

Satan causes delay so that he can remove a person from the timing of God's blessing. If Satan cannot destroy you, he will seek to delay you. When there is a delay, what do you do? Do you just keep waiting and watching the world pass you by? Or do you rise up, wait on the Lord, and watch and pray and fight while you are waiting to get understanding? You must develop spiritual discernment because your response to delay is very critical. You must know the source of the delay. King Saul learned this lesson the hard way.

In 1 Samuel 13, the Prophet Samuel delayed in coming to King Saul. Saul waited and Samuel did not come at the appointed time:

> [8] He waited seven days, the time set by Samuel; but Samuel did not come to Gilgal, and Saul's men began to scatter.
>
> [9] So he said, "Bring me the burnt offering and the fellowship offerings." And Saul offered up the burnt offering.
>
> [10] Just as he finished making the offering, Samuel arrived, and Saul went out to greet him.
>
> [11] "What have you done?" asked Samuel. Saul replied, "When I saw that the men were scattering, and that you did not come at the set time, and that the Philistines were assembling at Micmash,
>
> [12] I thought, 'Now the Philistines will come down against me at Gilgal, and I have not sought the Lord's favor.' So I felt compelled to offer the burnt offering."
>
> [13] "You acted foolishly," Samuel said. "You have not kept the command the Lord your God gave you; if you had, he would have established your kingdom over Israel for all time."

King Saul's failure to correctly respond to Samuel's delay cost him the kingship. Here, there was a divine delay that required King Saul to wait. The work of Satan is to get us to act (just like Sarah did with Hagar and Ishmael) when we ought to wait on the Lord. Divine delay as in the case of Samuel demands that we wait. Satanic delay demands that we rise up and fight.

The spirit of delay, such as the prince of Persia, is what Satan uses to introduce other spirits to afflict a believer or unbeliever. Delay is like a highway through which other demons gain access into the life of an individual. Once the spirit of delay gains ground in a person's life, if care is not taken that spirit will open the door for other spirits to enter and operate in that person's life.

Hope deferred makes the heart sick, but a longing fulfilled is a tree of life *(Prov. 13:12).*

The kingdom of darkness seeks to wear out people with delay because hope deferred makes the heart sick. If Satan can succeed in delaying you for a considerable period of time, your heart (spirit) will become sickened. Delay is a highway and many demons travel on this highway. If a person is expecting a blessing and there is a delay, especially a protracted delay, he must guard his heart to make sure delay does not bring in spirits of disappointment, frustration, discouragement, depression, bitterness, anger, accusation, murmuring, and a host of other wicked spirits.

When a person experiences a protracted delay, he starts becoming disappointed. The spirit of disappointment goes to work immediately to quench his expectations. The person may reduce his expectations as a coping mechanism to minimize the effects of disappointment. Continuous disappointment is designed to weaken the human spirit so that the person loses hope. This disappointment gains ground because of the spirit of delay. When hope is deferred, men are disappointed.

The spirit of delay is very wicked. In addition to opening the door to the spirit of disappointment, it allows in the spirit of frustration. There is the spirit of visible frustration and the spirit of silent frustration. With silent frustration, the victim cooperates with frustration and gives others the impression around him that all is alright. He continues like this, and if care is not taken, when he reaches the breaking point, he just snaps and people around him are surprised because they did not discern what was going on inside of him. With frustration easily comes the spirits of discouragement, bitterness, and anger. When there is delay and things are not going the way the person expected, bitterness and anger set in and begin to operate in that person's life. The person now has a short fuse and is ready to explode at the minimum provocation. If he does not guard his heart against the evil workings of Satan, he will take out his frustration on others by manifesting anger and bitterness and even jealousy.

When we are attacked by a spirit of delay we see our true character as believers. As soon as delay sets in, we must guard our heart from becoming sick. We must surrender our hearts to the Lord. With delay of blessings, we have seen people operate under a spirit of accusation. They begin to accuse God and their fellow man for their problems. They claim that if not for some man and if not for God being angry at them, they would not be in the mess they are in. The spirit of accusation belongs to the accuser in the midst of the brethren. If care is not taken, they also begin to light their own fires *(Isa. 50:11)*. They look for solutions to their problems outside of God. Delay brings frustration, and the spirit of frustration can cause someone to look for satanic assistance to solve a problem. Some have gone to satanic workers when looking for the fruit of the womb. They waited and waited for a baby that was not forthcoming and decided to use the services of a magician to conceive a baby. This is what the Bible means by lighting your own fire.

The person who has been driven to seek Satan's assistance as a result of his oppression is now not only incurring the wrath of God but inheriting more demons from the occult world. Now, through the workings of the spirit of delay, the kingdom of darkness has succeeded in establishing a college of demons in that person's life. The demons are laughing because they are yet to be challenged in their evil agenda and activities. Delay has succeeded in getting that person further away from God. If care is not taken, the person backslides. Lying spirits have now convinced him that it does not pay for him to serve God. The lying spirits tell him that even though God is said to be faithful, He is not and will not be faithful to him. This is why we must adopt a very violent warfare approach against the spirit of delay that seeks to impose a merciless satanic agenda against our lives.

Hope deferred makes the heart sick. Delay has a way of bringing in junk to the unguarded heart. The junk brought in by all manner of spirits associated with delay must be dealt with. God is a God of the heart, of the spirit. He wants to fellowship with that person in spirit but the spirit is sick. Only God can cleanse and deliver us from all the junk that Satan throws at us. Satan will throw junk at us if we allow him. That is why we must guard our hearts. Only God can deliver us from all the junk we pick up along life's journey. Satan seeks to populate the human heart with all manner of wickedness and wicked spirits so that his victims have difficulty relating to God through the Holy Spirit.

Satanic Covenant of Delay

The kingdom of darkness is well organized in terms of executing various evil programs upon humanity. When Satan wants to impose an agenda of delay in a person's life, he will assign a strong man. By terms of covenant, this strong man will be given the assignment of delay and will have other demonic powers carrying out his instructions and reporting to him. The strong man is given satanic authority and power to enforce delay by pulling back the hands of the clock supposed to be working in the favor of their victim. The strong man is quick to employ witches and wizards to carry out the terms of the covenant of delay. A coven of witches will gather where they will agree by covenant to harm their victim by enforcing delay in the victim's life. As the victim is battling various delays and being tormented by spirits assigned to enforce delay, these witches will be laughing in their secret meeting places.

For the covenant of delay to be effective, there often will be an agenda of delay. These evil powers enter into a covenant to inflict delay on a person in order to frustrate and torment that person. They will do everything to delay God's promises and prophecies from materializing in a person's life. To receive deliverance in this area, you must break evil covenants of delay in the name of Jesus Christ. You must remove yourself from the operation of the evil covenant by destroying all the terms and conditions of this covenant. The conditions of the covenant of demonic delay are often hinged on the victim succumbing to sin and not challenging its operation through getting violent *(Matt. 11:12)* with fasting, prayer, and spiritual warfare. The kingdom of darkness enjoys inflicting maximum damage on people with minimal interruption of their operations and activities. My prayer to God is that before I leave this earth he uses me to inflict maximum damage to the kingdom of darkness and to disrupt their operations and activities within my sphere of influence.

In that evil covenant of delay that recruits an army of demons reporting to the strong man of delay is provision for curses and afflictions. The curse of delay will make a person experience delays for years or a lifetime. Until that curse is broken and destroyed, one experiencing demonic delays will wrestle hard to gain a fraction of what is due to him. The blessing will come, but it will come very late. Delay is not necessarily denial, although in many instances it can result in denial. The curse of delay will permit the blessing to come when it is no longer necessary or when the victim is so worn out that he cannot even enjoy the blessing.

The evil covenant of delay always appoints a strong man to execute the agenda of delay. The function of that strong man is to defer hope and make the victim's heart sick. Many believers are tormented with a sick heart and are dying from it. Many believers are on antidepressants because of a sick heart. Others are threatening suicide. As mentioned earlier, delay is like a highway that many wicked spirits like to travel on to reach inside a man's heart and cause the heart to be sick. The spirit of suicide will work very hard to convince a person that his hope will never be realized and that life is not worth living. When a hope is deferred, we must as a matter of urgency guard our hearts. Powers of darkness rejoice every time a believer dies of a sick heart. We must learn to bind the strong man given the assignment of delay against us. We must begin to understand who our prince of Persia (delay) is and bind him.

In fact, no one can enter a strong man's house and carry off his possessions unless he first ties up the strong man. Then he can rob his house *(Mark 3:27).*

When you bind the strong man of delay effectively in the name of Jesus, you can now carry all his possessions that he trusted in and that he was using against you. Jesus is teaching us here that we must bind the strong man if we seek to plunder his house. The strong man is the devil's representative. We cannot become passive as believers to the extent that we fail to exercise our Christ-given authority to bind the strong man.

Types of Demonic Delays

1. Delay of Manifestations. Here a person has been waiting for the manifestation of God's Word in his life. He knows that God watches over His Word to perform it *(Jer. 1:12)* and yet the Word of God seems to be withheld by unexplainable circumstances. The strong man works to delay the manifestation as in the case of Daniel 10.

2. Delay of Expectations. Expectations are a strong belief that something will happen at an appointed time. There are realistic and unrealistic expectations. When a person has unrealistic expectations, he will require great faith and revelation from God concerning that expectation. Generally speaking, unrealistic expectations, apart from confirmation from God, will result in gross disappointment. Delay has a way of causing people to either change their expectations or become more realistic with a given expectation. Some have entered into marriage with the expectation that God will change their spouse. While God is not willing that any should perish and while God desires that all live a holy life and be blessed, that expectation may not even be in consonance with the Word of God that says not to be unequally yoked. The job of the strong man is to make sure that kind of expectation, nurtured outside the Word of God, is deferred and subsequently diminished.

3. Delay of Prophetic Fulfillment. The strong man works to delay the prophecies of God in our lives. He will do anything to get us off track so that the prophecy will linger as a result of our state of unpreparedness. The enemy will even bring false prophecies within our hearing so as to produce a state of confusion. When a person does not know what prophecy to believe, he lacks the faith to see the real thing come to pass. When the prophecy in question is to be fulfilled in our Canaan, the strong man will work on us being in Egypt at that time.

4. Delay of Destinies. In John 10:10, Jesus states that the thief comes only to steal and kill and destroy and that He came that we may have life and have life more abundantly. Satan is most interested in stealing destinies. Pharaoh, an agent of Satan in Exodus 1, sought to kill all the Hebrew boys at the moment of birth because he feared that their deliverance was at hand. Satan used Pharaoh to abort many destinies. In an attempt to ensure that the destiny of Jesus Christ did not come to fulfillment, Herod also sought to kill all the boys born in Bethlehem and its vicinity who were two years old and under. Satan will delay destiny to minimize the impact your destiny will have on the earth. The kingdom of heaven suffers violence, and the violent take it by force *(Matt. 11:12)*. We must fight to enter into our promise, into our destiny.

5. Delay in Communicating Divine Solutions. The strong man will delay God's clear divine instructions in order to introduce confusion. When instructions are delayed, we must wait on the Lord and not take matters into our own hands. The purpose of the delay is to get us to operate from a place of confusion instead of a place of confidence. When confusion sets in, it will work to bring in the spirit of doublemindedness. When doublemindedness comes, it comes with his companion, his twin spirit, which is the spirit of doubt. Many are waiting for God to speak, and God may indeed have spoken, but there could be a breakdown somewhere in the chain of communication. This again was the case with Daniel in Daniel 10.

6. Delay by Entanglements. This form of delay works to ensure that a person is entangled multiple times so that even when the strong man and other demonic powers are cast out, the effects of the entanglement remain to create further delay. It takes time to disentangle years of being stuck in a rut. Delays in financial blessings can expose one to lack and a spirit of poverty. Poverty eventually results in debt entanglement and further poverty. Some have been entangled by satanic-induced debts for decades. The burden of these debts have kept many on the sidelines and on the margins when they should have been at center stage, walking in the exciting destiny that God ordained for them.

7. Delays in Spiritual Warfare. In the course of spiritual warfare, the believer tends to get assistance from prayer warriors and intercessors. In spite of this great boost, the devil will work 'round the clock to drag the battle out for as long as possible. It may even seem like nothing is happening.
The Bible says one will chase a thousand, and two will put ten thousand to flight. As others intercede, the believer is getting the upper hand in the battle regardless of the delay.

> The war between the house of Saul and the house of David lasted a long time. David grew stronger and stronger, while the house of Saul grew weaker and weaker *(2 Sam. 3:1).*

The house of David was engaged in a long war. When the war gets long you must have endurance. War brings hardship and adjustments have to be made. In the course of this long war, David waxed stronger and stronger at the expense of the enemy. In spite of delays in the conclusion of your long drawn-out battle, you will grow stronger and stronger. The fact that you are getting stronger in the war does not mean that the war is over. Even though the house of Saul was growing weaker and weaker, it was still fighting David. The interesting thing about 2 Samuel 3 is that even though this long drawn-out war seems to be unending, David still receives his blessings from God. In the course of the war, David had sons born to him. David does not abandon family and social life because of the war. He is still fighting and still being blessed. The fact that there have been delays in the conclusion of the battle and that the enemy is still fighting you does not mean that you are disqualified from being blessed. The war should not hinder your blessing.

Nehemiah fought warfare against the enemies of Israel and built the walls of Jerusalem at the same time. The fight did not hinder him from doing the work of God. We cannot allow anything, including demonic delays, hinder us from doing God's work when we are in a position to carry out and continue with the work that God has called us to do. Instead of asking God to take you out of the battle, it makes more sense to ask Him to equip you for the battle that you have been called to fight in.

In Luke 18, Jesus tells the parable of the persistent widow and the unrighteous judge. The judge being unrighteous is one inspired by Satan. The persistent widow seeks justice from a satanic agent. Her justice is being delayed by the unrighteous judge. The spiritual strength of the widow lies in her persistent faith that eventually she will get her justice that has been denied her all the while. The widow did not sit at home waiting for justice. She kept going to the unrighteous judge to plead for justice against her adversary. Perhaps the widow in question lacked the means to appeal to a higher court of justice. However, unlike this widow, we have been afforded the means to appeal to the highest court: the courts of heaven where the Lord, the righteous Judge *(2 Tim. 4:8)*, sits in our favor. We must access the courts of heaven. The persistent widow could have waited at home, but she did not. You may be waiting on earth to get deliverance from your adversary and who knows, heaven may be waiting for you to confront that which needs to be confronted, just like the persistent widow. Seek and you shall find.

In Matthew 25, we see the parable of the ten virgins. Here, the bridegroom delayed:

The bridegroom was a long time in coming, and they all became drowsy and fell asleep *(Matt. 25:5)*.

The effect of the bridegroom's delay was to cause the ten virgins to become drowsy and fall asleep. That is what delay has the potential to do. However, it was the delay of the bridegroom that made it apparent that five of the virgins were foolish and five were wise. If the bridegroom had come on time, the foolish virgins may have had sufficient oil to meet the bridegroom. The foolish virgins had to go buy oil to meet the bridegroom, but while they were gone the bridegroom arrived and the door of the wedding banquet was shut. It is worthy to note that the foolish virgins went and bought the right thing. The problem was that they possessed the right thing (oil) at a time when it did not count. The foolish virgins did the right thing at the wrong time as a result of their being unprepared in the event that the bridegroom would tarry in coming. Not only did the bridegroom delay, the foolish virgins also suffered the result of their own delay and procrastination in getting oil at the time when they should have. Just like in this case, delay often works to bring the right thing at a time when its impact will be minimized. In this parable, the virgins who were ready went in with the bridegroom to the wedding banquet and then the door was shut. The door can be shut. The five foolish virgins were destined to be with the bridegroom, but the door was shut against them. There is a door of destiny that can be shut. Do not just assume that the door of destiny remains open at your convenience.

Delay works to keep a person on the same spot. The person will experience stagnation. Stagnation allows people who were way behind you to catch up with you and overtake you. When delay stagnates a person, the people he is supposed to be helping will be the ones extending help to him. The kingdom of darkness wants to keep many lives stagnated by delay.

Israel faced this problem of being stuck in the same spot in Deuteronomy 2:

You have circled this mountain long enough. Now turn north (*Deut. 2:3, NLT*).

God was telling the people not to keep wandering around the mountain and that it was time to move on. Sometimes because of the stigma caused by delay, certain mountains become our comfort zones and we are unwilling to take a step of faith and move on. Sometimes we become reluctant to leave that mountain, that secret place, because it has become our comfort zone where we receive sympathy and empathy.

The strong man knows that God loves His children and is working to deliver them. The attitude of the strong man in cases where God has a strong interest in a person is that "we know God loves him and that God will deliver him, but we will do everything to delay and drag out the deliverance as long as is possible." The delay will seek to convert itself into a permanent delay, which in effect is a denial.

In the course of our doing spiritual warfare and deliverance for Sister March, a demon manifested after much pressure and confessed that his assignment was to make sure Sister March never gets married. The demon became rather distraught and upset when we decreed in the name of Jesus that Sister March shall marry the man that God has appointed for her. The demon then spoke about how he had distracted and confused the man from realizing that Sister March was his wife. This type of demon sees prospective suitors as competition and will entangle them in a web of delay so that they are never ready to get married. Sister March's prospective husband must be discerning so that the strong man in her life does not direct him to the wrong woman or drag him down with all manner of delays.

When it comes to marriage, we must be extremely careful. If the kingdom of darkness succeeds in planting the wrong spouse in a person's life, that can cause serious delays to the working of God's plans for that person's life. The powers of darkness will use that wrong spouse as an agent to further delay God's divine purpose in that child of God's life. When he should be pursuing his destiny, he will be depleting his spiritual ammunition to fight matrimonial battles.

In conclusion, when faced with delays, we need to be discerning and ask the Lord for wisdom. Wisdom is supreme, and therefore we need wisdom. Though it costs all that one has, one must get understanding *(Prov. 4:7)*. Do not be like those that perish for lack of knowledge. As you stand fast in the Lord and walk in the Spirit, all things will work together for your good because of your love for God and because you are called according to His purpose. The enemy may delay your call that is according to God's purpose but so long as you love the Lord, the Bible says all things will turn out for good.

Prayers to Dismantle Demonic Delays

Meditate upon Psalm 70; Proverbs 13:12; Daniel 10; Mark 3:27; and Luke 18:1–8. The spirit of delay operates mainly in the heavenly realm and is a very stubborn and aggressive prince of darkness. To be effective, prayer should be done with fasting. Pray loud and with holy violence the following prayers:

1. In the name of Jesus Christ, I bind and overthrow every prince of darkness operating in the heavenly realms to detain the manifestation of my blessings and breakthrough.
2. In the name of Jesus, I release my prosperity, my health, my wealth, and my destiny that has been held back by witchcraft powers.
3. I bind the strong man supervising the detention of my blessings in the name of Jesus. Lord Jesus, I ask for angelic reinforcement to recover my blessings from the hand of the strong man and bring them to me speedily in Jesus' name.

4. In the name of Jesus, I cancel every demonic-induced delay upon my progress and ask that my steps be ordered only by the Lord.
5. I plead the blood of Jesus against spiritual forces of wickedness in high places that are conspiring to keep me in the same spot.
6. In the name of Jesus and by the power of the Holy Spirit, I clear my goods out of every satanic hiding place.
7. The God of Jehoshaphat that fought against the three nations, send confusion to the camp of my enemies that they may attack one another unto destruction in the name of Jesus.
8. Let the power of God destroy every covenant and agenda of delay working against my life in the name of Jesus.

4

BINDING AND LOOSING

In Matthew 16:19, in a conversation with Simon Peter, Jesus Christ says something rather profound:

> I will give you the keys of the kingdom of heaven; whatever you bind on earth will be bound in heaven, and whatever you loose on earth will be loosed in heaven.

The kingdom of heaven has keys. Keys indicate access. You need keys to access a facility. The keys to heaven grant you access to heaven and the things of heaven. To bind means to forbid, to lock, or to tie up. To loose means to allow, unlock, or untie. With keys you can lock (bind) and open (loose). Jesus has given us the keys of heaven. This is a great trust. You do not just give anyone your keys. You give your keys to people that you trust. You give your keys to competent people. You cannot give car keys to a ten year old. A ten year old is not competent and cannot be trusted to operate a motor vehicle.

The keys of heaven are not ordinary keys. These are spiritual keys. The keys are used on earth with heavenly implications. With the keys we can bind and loose on earth and it will be effected in the heavenly realms. Jesus, in giving the keys of heaven to Simon Peter, made him an authorized user of the keys of heaven. In Matthew 16:19, Jesus Christ speaks specifically to Simon Peter and gives him the keys of heaven. In Matthew 18:18, the keys are given to the disciples of Jesus Christ.

> I tell you the truth, whatever you bind on earth will be bound in heaven, and whatever you loose on earth will be loosed in heaven *(Matt. 18:18)*.

There are certain things on earth that are running loose and that need to be bound. They run loose on earth and affect destinies in the heavenly realm. Revelation 12:12 reports that Satan and his demons were cast down to earth, filled with fury. They are running loose on the earth and need to be bound in the name of Jesus. Satan is a thief and the thief comes to steal, kill, and destroy *(John 10:10)*. We cannot allow a thief to be on the loose. Even in human society, thieves are not left on the loose. When caught, they are handcuffed (bound) in order to protect society. Satan and his demons are destroyers and so with the keys of heaven, we must bind them here on earth and keep them bound in the heavenly realms. If you do not bind a destroyer, you give that destroyer the opportunity to bind you and if care is not taken, destroy you. You must bind the enemy before he binds you.

Samson sought revenge against the Philistines in Judges 15:1–5. Here is the account of what Samson did:

> ¹ Later on, at the time of wheat harvest, Samson took a young goat and went to visit his wife. He said, "I'm going to my wife's room." But her father will not let him go in.
>
> ² "I was so sure you thoroughly hated her," he said, "that I gave her to your friend. Isn't her younger sister more attractive? Take her instead."

³ Samson said to them, "This time I have a right to get even with the Philistines; I will really harm them."

⁴ So he went out and caught three hundred foxes and tied them tail to tail in pairs. He then fastened a torch to every pair of tails,

⁵ Lit the tails and let the foxes loose in the standing grain of the Philistines. He burned up the shocks and standing grain, together with the vineyards and olive groves.

Samson lets three hundred foxes loose burning with fire to destroy Philistine property. If the Philistines had had the ability to bind these three hundred foxes before they got to their vineyards and farms, these foxes would not have been able to inflict damage. Many times as Christians, we have the authority to bind foxes before they get to us, but we remain passive. If the Philistines bound the foxes while they were in their vineyards, what difference would it have made? The vineyard would have still been destroyed because the foxes got there before action was taken. As a believer, you must bind the foxes before they get to you. It is the little foxes that spoil the vine *(Song of Sol. 2:15)*, and so you must bind them even before they get to your vine (your blessing). In this sense, binding is a preventive measure. You bind the devourer before he can strike. Foxes, like demons, are destroyers, and so we must bind them. In the same way that Samson set foxes loose to destroy the blessings of the Philistines, Satan has set demons loose to destroy your blessings. You must bind these demons before they get to your blessings. When you bind something, you tie it up hand and foot, and it cannot move any longer according to its desire.

The kingdom of darkness works to keep blessings and treasures of ours bound. It is also for this reason that Jesus gave us the keys of heaven, the master keys to unlock that which is bound and to lock up (bind) that which needs to be restrained from committing further havoc. Some people are struggling with spirits of addiction that keep them bound through uncontrollable cravings for harmful substances.

Likewise, there are things on earth that the enemy has bound that need to be loosed. Until these things are loosed, they will remain tied up. The devil has a tendency to bind the things that we need to help us reach our destiny. Satan will bind, and if need be, delay our destiny helpers until we get into a rut.

Jesus Christ was destined to enter Jerusalem triumphantly riding on the back of a colt *(Zech. 9:9)*. The colt that was destined to carry Jesus Christ to Jerusalem had been bound in a nearby village *(Luke 19:30)*. When a person is bound, he remains in the same spot until he is loosed. Similarly, when you bind a demon in the name of Jesus, it remains bound in the same spot until it is cast out or, hopefully not, released. Until your "colt" is loosed, you cannot get to your Jerusalem. Your colt is that which is needed to get you to your place of destiny. The enemy has tied down many of the things that God may have appointed to help get us to our next level. We need to engage in spiritual warfare and untie that which has been tied by the enemy. You can command the forces of darkness to release their grip and hold over your blessings.

> As he approached Bethphage and Bethany at the hill called the Mount of Olives, he sent two of his disciples, saying to them, "Go to the village ahead of you, and as you enter it, you will find a colt tied there, which no one has ever ridden. Untie it and bring it here. If anyone asks you, 'Why are you untying it?' tell him, 'The Lord needs it" *(Luke 19:29–31)*.

Jesus instructed his disciples to untie that which was tied because he had need of it. What do you have need of that has been tied down by dark powers in the heavenly realm? Is it a job? Is it healing? Loose those things now on earth and they shall be loosed in heaven. Daniel's answer in Daniel 10 was bound by the prince of Persia for twenty-one days. Angelic reinforcement released the answer to Daniel.

Do not think that because you are a Christian you cannot be bound by Satan. This is warfare. Satan and his demons are also doing some evil binding and evil loosing. In Luke 13:10–16, there was a woman who had a spirit of infirmity:

10 On a Sabbath Jesus was teaching in one of the synagogues,

11 and a woman was there who had been crippled by a spirit for eighteen years. She was bent over and could not straighten up at all.

12 When Jesus saw her, he called her forward and said to her, "Woman, you are set free from your infirmity."

13 Then he put his hands on her, and immediately she straightened up and praised God.

14 Indignant because Jesus had healed on the Sabbath, the synagogue ruler said to the people, "There are six days for work. So come and be healed on those days, not on the Sabbath."

15 The Lord answered him, "You hypocrites! Doesn't each of you on the Sabbath untie his ox or donkey from the stall and lead it out to give it water?

16 Then should not this woman, a daughter of Abraham, whom Satan has kept bound for eighteen long years, be set free on the Sabbath day from what bound her?"

This woman was a daughter of Abraham, a child of faith, and yet she was bound by Satan for eighteen long years. Whom the Son sets free is free indeed *(John 8:36)*. Many Christians are bound and trapped by sin, by infirmity, by poverty, by demons, and by their carnal fleshly desires. Christians have been given the keys to bind and loose and must loose themselves from these demonic entanglements and hindrances just like Jesus did unto the believer that was bound by a spirit of infirmity for eighteen years.

Matthew 18:18 makes it clear that whatsoever we loose on earth is loosed in heaven. If it is not loosed in heaven, then all our loosing on earth is in vain. If it is not loosed in heaven that may mean that we may be using the wrong set of keys on earth. Heaven backs us up when we bind and loose in the name of Jesus.

Matthew 18:19 shows that our binding and loosing is based on agreement. What is happening today is that in a given situation, one believer is binding and another believer is loosing what his fellow believer has bound. Agreement is lacking. In summer 2015, I recall a conversation I had on a public bus with a fellow Christian. He posited that as Christians we must be tolerant and approve of same-sex marriages because we are all children of God. As I listened to him, I was reminded of all my prayers that homosexual and lesbian spirits be bound in our churches and ministries so that believers can be presented pure in Christ. Here I was binding these demonic spirits and my fellow believer was busy loosing them without understanding the spiritual implications of what he was saying.

> Again, I tell you that if two of you on earth agree about anything you ask for, it will be done for you by my Father in heaven *(Matt. 18:19)*.

Agreement is critical in spiritual warfare. The devil works so hard to make Christians disagree. Broadly speaking, there are two types of disagreements: (i) outright disagreement and (ii) lack of agreement. The latter may be worse because a lack of agreement is a breeding ground for confusion.

Satan will do everything to make sure that believers do not agree, because if we can touch and agree on earth, we will adversely affect the kingdom of darkness. Satan keeps believers busy so that they do not even have time to meet and agree. So long as believers fail to agree, the kingdom of darkness will have free reign over many situations affecting our world.

Binding Powers of Darkness

> Or else how can one enter into a strong man's house, and spoil his goods, except he first bind the strong man? And then he will spoil his house *(Matt. 12:29, KJV)*.

> No man can enter into a strong man's house, and spoil his goods, except he will first bind the strong man; and then he will spoil his house *(Mark 3:27, KJV)*.

> When a strong man, fully armed, guards his own house, his possessions are safe. But when someone stronger attacks and overpowers him, he takes away the armor in which the man trusted and divides up the spoils *(Luke 11:20–22)*.

The Bible talks about binding the strong man. Therefore, it is important that we know how to identify who the strong man is in every situation. As the name implies, the strong man has power. The Bible says the strong man has a house and that he guards it. In the house of the strong man are his possessions, which he has appropriated from his victims over a considerable period of time. From the above Scriptures we also see that the strong man has an armor to defend himself against attacks. The strong man is an agent of Satan whose mission is to further the agenda of Satan. To be effective against the strong man, Jesus stated that we must first bind him. Merely saying "I bind you, strong man" does not necessarily bind the strong man. He has an armor that can stand the power of your attempt to bind him. The seven sons of Sceva found that out the hard way in Acts 19. Their words were empty, and their attempt to cast out a demon proved catastrophic. The strong man that operated against Daniel in Daniel 10 was the prince of Persia. He operated in the heavenly realm against Daniel. Jesus encountered the strong man in his ministry of deliverance.

Mark 5:1–15:

¹ They went across the lake to the region of the Gerasenes.

² When Jesus got out of the boat, a man with an impure spirit came from the tombs to meet him.

³ This man lived in the tombs, and no one could bind him anymore, not even with a chain.

⁴ For he had often been chained hand and foot, but he tore the chains apart and broke the irons on his feet. No one was strong enough to subdue him.

⁵ Night and day among the tombs and in the hills he would cry out and cut himself with stones.

⁶ When he saw Jesus from a distance, he ran and fell on his knees in front of him.

⁷ He shouted at the top of his voice, "What do you want with me, Jesus, Son of the Most High God? In God's name don't torture me!"

⁸ For Jesus had said to him, "Come out of this man, you impure spirit!"

⁹ Then Jesus asked him, "What is your name?"

"My name is Legion," he replied, "for we are many."

¹⁰ And he begged Jesus again and again not to send them out of the area.

¹¹ A large herd of pigs was feeding on the nearby hillside.

¹² The demons begged Jesus, "Send us among the pigs; allow us to go into them."

¹³ He gave them permission, and the impure spirits came out and went into the pigs. The herd, about two thousand in number, rushed down the steep bank into the lake and were drowned.

¹⁴ Those tending the pigs ran off and reported this in the town and countryside, and the people went out to see what had happened.

¹⁵ When they came to Jesus, they saw the man who had been possessed by the legion of demons, sitting there, dressed and in his right mind; and they were afraid.

When the demons are confronted by Jesus, one of them answers on behalf of the rest. He identifies himself as Legion and says that they are many. This is the strong man speaking for the others. He is pleading with Jesus not to torment him, and yet he was tormenting his victim.

The strong man asked Jesus for mercy, but he was unwilling to show mercy to his victim. Legion was the strong man but Jesus is the stronger man *(Luke 11:20–22).*

When Brother April came to our ministry, he had been bogged down by failures and delays emanating from the strong man of his father's house. This ancestral ruling spirit had put his destiny on hold. As soon as the Lord revealed what the problem was, we began aggressively binding the strong man of Brother April's father's house. The strong man had caused so much strife and mistrust in the family and was unwilling to allow Brother April to reach a particular milestone toward his destiny. The strong man had arrested the destinies of many in this family and even aborted some destinies. With warfare prayers and our continuous binding of the strong man, Brother April's delayed achievements were released from the house of the strong man. Brother April got the victory after several years of being denied by the strong man.

This strong man is seen again in Isaiah 49:24–26:

> 24 Can plunder be taken from warriors, or captives rescued from the fierce?
>
> 25 But this is what the Lord says: "Yes, captives will be taken from warriors, and plunder retrieved from the fierce; I will contend with those who contend with you, and your children I will save.
>
> 26 I will make your oppressors eat their own flesh; they will be drunk on their own blood, as with wine. Then all mankind will know that I, the Lord, am your Savior, your Redeemer, the Mighty One of Jacob."

The Bible here is calling the strong man a warrior, a fierce one that keeps captives and plunder. The King James Version refers to the strong man as "the mighty" and "the terrible." He is mighty but he is not the Almighty. As strong as the strong man is, he can be bound. Once he is bound, a person can be assured of his deliverance. The strong man is the one that stands in the way to frustrate deliverance. The strong man may not necessarily be the first to manifest in deliverance, and while we may be casting out the demons that first manifest, the strong man remains in the house organizing the frustration of a well-meaning deliverance. This is why Jesus tells us that we must first bind him before we do anything else. Until the strong man is bound, we cannot plunder his house. What sometimes happens is that when certain demons are cast out and the strong man is still in the house, those demons that were cast out will come back. Unless the strong man is bound effectively, he will open the doors for other evil spirits to return.

How do we bind the strong man? Do we bind him by merely saying, "Strong man, I bind you in the name of Jesus"? Binding the strong man requires a display of strength. Luke 11:22 says that a stronger man is needed to bind the strong man. The One stronger than the strong man is Jesus Christ. Jesus Christ has given us power and authority to bind the strong man. The weapon that Jesus recommends against the strong man is binding. Now, the weapons of our warfare are not carnal but are mighty through God to the pulling down of strongholds. We have been given mighty weapons in Christ that we must use to arrest the strong man and keep him bound. The way to bind the strong man is to use the power given by the stronger man, Jesus Christ. You cannot use the power of Jesus Christ if you are not totally yielded and submitted to Jesus Christ. The power of Jesus Christ calls for violence. Violence in fasting, in prayer, in warfare, and in determination to see the strong man bound and defeated, and to top it all by plundering his goods.

> And from the days of John the Baptist until now the kingdom of heaven suffereth violence, and the violent take it by force (Matt. 11:12, KJV).

You must be violent and take what heaven has given you by force. Your blessings bestowed by heaven must not remain in the house of the strong man. The kingdom of heaven forcefully advances when believers become violent in their warfare against the strong man.

There are various strong men assigned by Satan to different spheres of life. A strong man is assigned to individuals, families, organizations, businesses, government departments, ministries, churches, cities, states, and nations.

Nowhere in the Bible are we told that we can bind Satan. We are told to submit to God and resist the devil and he will flee. Attempting to bind Satan would amount to what Paul calls beating the air in 1 Corinthians 9:26. If we could bind Satan, all the problems we are experiencing would be over. Luke 10:19 gives us authority over all the power of the enemy, and this is the case considering that greater is the One that is in us than he that is in the world. Nonetheless, Satan's evil activities have been predetermined by God, and we are not in a position to bind him and hinder him from roaming the earth. It is presumptuous to think we can bind him when God never expressly says so. On the other hand, Jesus tells us that the spirits are subject to us *(Luke 10:20)*, and he gives us authority to cast out demons. Mark 16:17 confirms this as being one of the signs of a true believer.

Many in Christendom have questioned the practice of binding demons and the strong man. In Luke 10:19, Jesus gave believers power and authority to tread on snakes and scorpions and over all the power of the enemy with the assurance that nothing shall by any means hurt us. Again, Mark 16:17 mentions the casting out of devils as a sign that follows the believer. If a demon can be cast out in the name of Jesus, then surely it can be bound in the name of Jesus. In Acts 16:18, Paul cast out a spirit of divination from a young girl. In the gospels, Jesus makes it clear that concerning the strong man, we must first bind him. Christ has given us authority to bind and loose in his name. Those that question whether this is so will have to look at the New Testament as a whole.

> Verily, verily, I say unto you, He that believeth on me, the works that I do shall he do also; and greater works than these shall he do; because I go unto my Father. **And whatsoever ye shall ask in my name, that I will do**, that the Father may be glorified in the Son *(John 14:12–13)*.

I have highlighted the above phrase in John 14:13 to show that in this warfare, an element of great faith is involved. If you do not believe that you can ask that a demon be bound in Jesus' name, then Jesus is not obligated to effect the binding.

If evil spirits can be bound, wouldn't that mean that spirits of God can be loosed? I will examine the Scriptures and also share our ministry experience in answering this question.

Loosing Spirits of God

In Hebrews 1:14, referring to angels, it is stated that angels are ministering spirits, sent forth to minister for them who shall be heirs of salvation. In other words, angels minister on behalf of believers. God has spirits (angels) working for the heirs of salvation (believers). 1 John 4:1 urges us not to believe every spirit but to try the spirits to see whether they are of God. This means that in our walk here on earth, we may encounter spirits and when we do so we must try them to see whether they are of God or not. If they are of God, they are to minister for us.

Since we have established by Scripture that we have ministering spirits, can we loose them to fight in spiritual warfare on our behalf?

The Apostle Paul in his epistle to the church in Ephesus had this to say in Ephesians 1:15–17, KJV:

[15] Wherefore I also, after I heard of your faith in the Lord Jesus, and love unto all the saints,

[16] Cease not to give thanks for you, making mention of you in my prayers,

[17] That the God of our Lord Jesus Christ, the Father of glory, may give unto you the spirit of wisdom and revelation in the knowledge of Him.

Here, Paul was praying to God to release the spirit of wisdom and revelation to believers in Ephesus.

In our deliverance ministry, as we have asked in the name of Jesus for a release of warrior angels from God to assist us in the deliverance, we have seen the tables turn in our favor. We have asked ministering spirits from God to help us, and they did compel the demons we were facing to depart from their victim. If we can hinder ministering spirits from helping us, we can also facilitate their helping us in warfare and deliverance. Why would any believer believe this is not the position? We need faith to harness all that we have been given in Christ Jesus. If you do not know what you have been given, you will not be able to possess your possession.

Christ has given us the power to bind and loose—to use it to wage war against the kingdom of darkness.

Binding and Loosing Prayers

Meditate upon the following Scriptures: Matthew 11:12; Matthew 16:19; Mark 3:27; Luke 11:20–22; and Isaiah 49:24–26. Pray the following prayers authoritatively and in faith:

1. I bind every strong man assigned and operating against me in the name of Jesus.
2. I bind every evil spirit in the heavenly realms that is working to frustrate my life in the name of Jesus.
3. I bind witchcraft powers, occult powers, and territorial demons, ancestral powers of my father's house, and ancestral powers of my mother's house in the name of Jesus Christ.
4. I bind and receive deliverance from the spirits of rejection, bitterness, rebellion, anger, and trauma in the name of Jesus.
5. I bind every power that has bound me and command them to release me now by fire in the name of Jesus. I break every satanic chain upon my life in the name of Jesus.

6. With the keys of the kingdom of Heaven and in the name of Jesus, I bind the strong man working against my health, my career, my marriage, my family, and my destiny in the name of Jesus.

7. Heavenly Father, I ask in the name of Jesus that you release, loose, and send forth ministering spirits to fight against every demonic power that has arisen against me.

8. Lord in the name of Jesus, send forth unto me the Spirit of the Lord, the Spirit of wisdom, the Spirit of understanding, the Spirit of counsel and of power, the Spirit of knowledge and of fear of the Lord.

9. With the keys of heaven and in the name of Jesus, I open every satanic padlock and chain that is withholding my blessings and virtues.

5

ENGAGING AND DEFEATING POWERS OF DARKNESS

God raised up Joshua as the leader of Israel to succeed Moses. Joshua was given the task of leading the Israelites to possess land in the occupation of enemies. He was bound to meet stiff opposition and resistance from within his camp and from the camps of various enemies. To defeat his enemies and succeed, God instructed Joshua to be strong, very courageous, and obedient *(Josh. 1:7)*. So long as Joshua heeded the instructions in Joshua 1:7, he was sure to defeat all powers that he had to engage.

When it was time to confront the enemies occupying the territories that God promised the Israelites, Joshua did not just go out with his army without doing sufficient research. In Joshua 2, Joshua secretly sent two spies to look over the land, especially Jericho. The purpose of secretly sending out spies was to get the necessary information to wage a successful warfare. Fact finding is crucial in defeating the enemy. You must know their strengths and weaknesses. Joshua sent out the spies in secret. When you are gathering information in warfare, you must be discreet. The spies came back to Joshua, not only with the facts but with the right conclusion.

Then the two men started back. They went down out of the hills, forded the river, and came to Joshua son of Nun, and told him everything that had happened to them. They said to Joshua, "The Lord has surely given the whole land into our hands; all the people are melting in fear because of us" *(Josh. 2:23–24).*

The spies told Joshua everything. When you are engaging and fighting the enemy, you need to learn as much as possible about him. The Bible teaches us a lot about the character of Satan and his host of demons. It tells us that Satan is a thief, murderer, destroyer *(John 10:10)*, liar *(John 8:44)*, accuser in the midst of the brethren *(Rev. 12:10)*, tormentor *(Matt. 18:34)*, prince of the air *(Eph. 2:2)*, deceiver *(Rev. 12:9)* that can appear as an angel of light *(2 Cor. 11:14)*, etc. The Bible tells us about his satanic network and hierarchy that comprises principalities and powers, rulers of the darkness of this world, and spiritual wickedness in high places *(Eph. 6:12)*. It helps to know who the enemy is and what he is not so that you do not waste valuable time and strength fighting the wrong enemy and the wrong battle. Joshua knew who he was and who God was. In addition to knowing your enemy's capabilities, you must know who you are and who Christ is. In addition, you should know why Jesus came to earth and why he returned to heaven: to destroy the works of the devil *(1 John 3:8)* and to save man *(John 3:16)*. God had given Joshua the assurance that He would be with Joshua. Just like Joshua, we must know the spiritual power, authority, and weapons that we have been given in Christ Jesus.

In Luke 9:1, Jesus called his twelve disciples together and gave them power and authority over all devils and to cure diseases—in short, they were given the power and authority to provide deliverance and healing. To engage powers of darkness and defeat them in battle, you must have authority and power. The power we have over the enemy flows from God's authority. Authority can exist without power, and power can exist without authority. They are two separate yet interrelated concepts. Authority gives you the right to exercise power. Power is the ability to get a task done. In 1 Samuel 13:8–14, King Saul exercised power to perform a priestly function, but he had no authority to do so and so he was punished.

As Christians, we have been given authority, yet many Christians are powerless. Christians must walk in the consciousness that they can do all things that God has willed for them to do through Christ that strengthens them *(Phil. 4:13)*. In Exodus 4, God gives Moses authority to represent Him before Pharaoh. In Exodus 4:17, God gives Moses a staff with power to perform miraculous signs. If someone other than Moses were to have attempted to use Moses's staff, that would have been an unauthorized use of power with costly consequences.

In Luke 10:19, Jesus gives authority (NLT, New International Version, and New King James Version) to his disciples to trample on snakes and scorpions and to overcome all the power of the enemy. Jesus assures them that nothing shall by any means harm them. The King James Version uses the word "authority" in place of power. In short, this authority and power was given to us to trample on snakes and scorpions. Snakes and scorpions are not to trample upon us. We as believers are to trample upon them. If snakes and scorpions are trampling upon you, if the power of the enemy is harming you, then you are in need of deliverance.

As believers, God has given us the authority and the power to engage the powers of darkness, defeat them, bind them, and cast them out. You have the authority, but are you exercising the power? If you do have the power and are exercising it, is your power sufficient?

In Matthew 17:14–21, the disciples' lack of prayer and fasting minimized their power over the enemy. The disciples had the authority to cast out the demon from the boy but were unable to do so. Jesus had given them authority to cast out demons, yet in this case, the corresponding power was lacking. Earlier on, we defined power as the ability to get a task done. Here, they were unable to drive out a demon, and so the task remained undone. The disciples inquired of Jesus about their inability to drive out the demon. Jesus told them that it was because they had so little faith. They had faith, but it was not sufficient. They had power, but it was not enough because the type of demon they were dealing with only went out by fasting and prayer. Their unbelief depreciated their power.

Any time power is given, it is given for a purpose. So far we have seen in Luke 9:1 and Luke 10:19 that power was given to believers to defeat demons. The signs mentioned in Mark 16:17–18 are the evidence of this power. When these signs accompany your walk, it shows that you are walking in the authority and power that only Christ confers.

> And these signs will accompany those who believe: In my name they will drive out demons; they will speak in new tongues; they will pick up snakes with their hands; and when they drink deadly poison, it will not hurt them at all; they will place their hands on sick people, and they will get well *(Mark 16:17–18)*.

Power is mentioned again in Acts 1:8, KJV: "But ye shall receive power after that the Holy Ghost is come upon you and ye shall be witnesses unto me both in Jerusalem and in all Judea and in Samaria and unto the uttermost part of the earth." The purpose of the power in Acts 1:8 is to enable a disciple of Christ to become a witness for Christ. To effectively fight darkness, you must be a witness of the light. You must be an effective witness for Jesus Christ. The power given at Pentecost with the evidence of speaking in tongues is the power to witness for Christ. Prior to this power being released, Simon Peter was quick to deny Christ at the inquiry of the authorities. After Pentecost in Acts 2, we see Simon

Peter witness for Christ with authority, power, and boldness. A witness for Christ lives a life that reflects Christlikeness and is empowered to walk in holiness. A witness speaks. As we preach the gospel of Jesus Christ, enemy strongholds are broken down and captives are set free.

One should not attempt or profess to use the power of Christ if he lacks the authority to do so. If you are not a believer, if you have not surrendered your life to Christ, it is futile to engage powers of darkness in warfare. The seven sons of a Jewish chief priest learned a hard lesson in Acts 19:13–16:

> 13 Some Jews who went around driving out evil spirits tried to invoke the name of the Lord Jesus over those who were demon-possessed. They would say, "In the name of the Jesus whom Paul preaches, I command you to come out."
>
> 14 Seven sons of Sceva, a Jewish chief priest, were doing this.
>
> 15 One day the evil spirit answered them, "Jesus I know, and Paul I know about, but who are you?"
>
> 16 Then the man who had the evil spirit jumped on them and overpowered them all. He gave them such a beating that they ran out of the house naked and bleeding.

The demon in the man overpowered the sons of Sceva to the point where they had to flee, naked and bleeding. Demons have this kind of power to afflict and torment but greater is the One that is in us than he that is in the world. The seven sons of Sceva were not authorized to use the power in the name of Jesus to engage the enemy. They paid a steep price. The seven sons of Sceva played with fire, and they got burnt. Demons do not flee from anyone who does not know Jesus or who is not spiritually prepared. To be ready to fight in the spiritual battles against powers of darkness, we must get real with God.

It is pertinent to note the following points relating to the seven sons of Sceva's experience in Acts 19:

1. The demon knew who the true believers were that it had to watch out for. If you truly live for Jesus, Satan's kingdom will be threatened by your warfare.

2. Merely praying in Jesus' name like Sceva's sons did is not enough to defeat powers of darkness. You must be submitted to His name. "In the name of Jesus" is not a mantra. In Matthew 7:21, Jesus cautions that not all that says to him, "Lord, Lord," will enter the kingdom of heaven, but only he that does the will of his Father in heaven. Merely naming Jesus is not a substitute for knowing him.

3. The seven sons of Sceva could copy Paul's words but not his power acquired through his personal relationship with God. You can duplicate the words and deeds of an anointed man of God but you cannot receive the benefit of his walk with God. Christian maturity takes effort and comes with time.

4. Imitating the faith of others cannot give you the victory.

5. The seven sons of Sceva can be likened to the five foolish virgins in Matthew 25. You cannot depend on others' oil for your salvation.

6. Like Paul, the moment you have a genuine life-changing encounter with Jesus Christ, the kingdom of darkness is aware.

7. You cannot use the carnal weapons of flesh and blood to wrestle with principalities and powers.

From way back in the book of Genesis, God has been telling His people that they will possess the gates of their enemies *(Gen. 22:17)*. It is worthy to note that possessing the enemy's gates is an uphill task when the enemy is in control and in possession of your own gates. The gates regulate the flow of traffic and the flow of blessings. The enemy has possessed the gates of some believers. The devil, through a spirit of fear and intimidation, accusation, and condemnation, and other means, succeeds in controlling what some believers do and do not do, where they go and cannot go. Do not listen to the enemy. Listen to God! In such a situation, Jesus owns the believer, yet the enemy is controlling and manipulating his life. The believer in this situation needs to first recover his gates from the hand of the enemy before he can possess the gates of his own enemies. The good news is that God has made provision through deliverance and healing to ensure that the enemy does not enforce and maintain a monopoly of dominion over God's children.

> The scepter of the wicked will not remain over the land allotted to the righteous, for then the righteous might use their hands to do evil *(Ps. 125:3)*.

The scepter of the wicked refers to the enemy's authority. The land allotted to the righteous refers to the portion and blessings of the believer. The Word of God is saying here that the power of the enemy, the powers of darkness, will not be allowed to rule and reign over your blessings so that you are not tempted to iniquity. The Word of God is saying that enough is enough—no more enemy dominion over your life. The devices of Satan will not be allowed to oppress our lives any longer, and so to stop the enemy, God has given us weapons of warfare, which are not of this world, but which are mighty through God to the pulling down of strongholds *(2 Cor. 10:3–5)*. You must use your spiritual weapons in conjunction with the whole armor of God *(Eph. 6:10–18)* to engage the powers of darkness and to bind them, resist them, cast them out, and put them to flight in the name of Jesus.

It is critical to our victory that we are in submission to God's authority. You cannot afford to be in rebellion or disobedience and defeat the dark powers that are fighting you. When you submit to God, you are under his authority and so He will give you power to resist the devil and the devil will flee (*James 4:7*). All authority emanates from God. If you are not in submission to established authority on earth, then you are not submitted to God.

Permit me to digress a little bit with this illustration, which I hope you will find somewhat pertinent: The United States Constitution prescribes and defines a separation of powers for the three arms of government. Congress, being the lawmaker, reflects God. The president, charged with executing the provisions of the law, reflects the believer. The judiciary, adjudicating and passing judgment, reflects God, the righteous Judge of 2 Timothy 4:8.

Under the US Constitution, Congress declares war and authorizes the president in his capacity as commander-in-chief to fight war. The president (just like we believers) has been given the power to wage war but the authority to do so resides with Congress (just like God). Hence, Congress gives the president the authority to fight war. When occasion demands, the president as commander-in-chief may launch a preemptive strike and seek support from Congress afterward. Let's stretch this a bit further to gain understanding of management of warfare.

US President Harry S. Truman did not seek a formal declaration from Congress to enter into the Korean War. The Korean War of 1950 was a war, but the US decided to call it a conflict to avoid going through congressional questioning, scrutiny, debating, and approvals. Hence, when the president as commander-in-chief acts in this manner (by calling acts of war a conflict or preemptive strike), his actions raise serious constitutional concerns. However, as believers, we are in a better position than the US president. Jesus Christ has already given us the authority and the power we need to wage war against Satan and his network of demonic beings.

A few days after the September 11, 2001, attacks in America, the US Congress gave the president global powers to fight terrorism. Congress passed AUMF (Authorization for Use of Military Force), giving the president in his capacity as commander-in-chief the authority to use all necessary and appropriate force against the perpetrators of the September 11 attacks on America. In similar fashion, Satan and his demons are terrorists and Christ has given us spiritual authority and power against them. They were defeated in a war that broke out in heaven, and it is our duty to defeat them on earth in the name of Jesus.

In the battle we are called to fight with darkness, we must not cut corners by hoping to compromise with darkness to get respite from darkness. Do not trade with the enemy—that is a war crime. Fight the enemy and defeat the enemy in Jesus' name. No negotiation, no retreat, no surrender in Jesus' name.

Now that we appreciate the importance of fighting spiritual warfare from a position of power and authority, let us examine the weapons that we have in Christ to defeat powers of darkness.

For as he thinks in his heart, so is he *(Prov. 23:7, NKJV).*

Satanic powers work very hard to control and manipulate people's minds in order to get entrenched in their souls. If Satan can control the way a believer thinks, he can exert dominion over virtually every area of that believer's life. This is why we must be continuously transformed by the renewing of our minds *(Rom. 12:2).* Demons work on planting lies in the minds of believers and then making them strongholds.

I remember praying and doing deliverance for a precious sister over the phone. She was fully convinced that Christ had condemned her because she heard voices that kept telling her that this was so. All my efforts to convince her otherwise proved abortive as she was apparently under the control of a mind-control spirit and a host of other demons. As believers, we must rid ourselves of all strongholds planted by the enemy in our thought processes. As a man thinks, so is he. Do not let the enemy influence or control your thinking. If Satan controls a person's thinking, he will block the person from receiving truth. God has provided mighty weapons to help rid us of Satan's lies and propaganda so we can properly wage war against him and defeat him *(2 Cor. 10:3–5)*.

Repentance

In our battle with the forces of darkness, we must confess and repent of all known sin.

> If we claim to be without sin, we deceive ourselves and the truth is not in us. If we confess our sins, he is faithful and just and will forgive us our sins and purify us from all unrighteousness. If we claim we have not sinned, we make him out to be a liar and his word has no place in our lives *(1 John 1:8–10)*.

The above Scripture makes it clear that if we deny our sins, the truth of God is not in us. If we confess our sins, God will forgive us and cleanse us from all unrighteousness. We always want the truth of God to be in us and to never be lacking in us. Holding on to sin deprives us from living in the truth. The function of confession and repentance is to make us forsake our evil ways and bring us into alignment with God's truth. We cannot fight the father of lies when we ourselves are living a lie. In any area of unconfessed sin, Satan will use such an area to develop a stronghold that he can use as his defense against our attacks.

Repentance is more than turning a new leaf or being sorry. A drastic U-turn from anything that is sinful is required. Godly sorrow and repentance is critical to deliverance and for waging spiritual warfare. We must repent of any unforgiveness and bitterness toward others. One of the deadliest weapons that Satan deploys to hinder our spiritual growth is unforgiveness, a sin that puts people in bondage and hinders the flow of the power of God needed to engage the powers of darkness. Unforgiveness questions your authority and power base in spiritual warfare. Those who refuse to let go of their hate, anger, resentment, and bitterness give enormous ground to the enemy and only genuine repentance from these toxic and contaminating sins can put one in right standing to wage war against Satan and demons.

> And when ye stand praying forgive, if ye have aught against any: that your Father also which is in heaven may forgive you your trespasses. But if ye do not forgive, neither will your Father which is in heaven forgive your trespasses *(Mark 11:25–26, KJV).*

One of the true indications of spiritual maturity is the ability to easily forgive and let go. As we have received forgiveness from God through our Lord Jesus Christ, we are called to show mercy to those that offended us by forgiving them. This also is a mark of humility.

> Get rid of all bitterness, rage and anger, brawling and slander, along with every form of malice. Be kind and compassionate to one another, forgiving each other, just as in Christ God forgave you *(Eph. 4:31–32).*

The Word of God

Another mighty weapon of warfare in the arsenal of the believer is the sword of the Spirit, the Word of God *(Eph. 6:17)*. The Word of God embodies truth. Jesus is the Word *(John 1:1–14)* and in John 14:6, Christ defines Himself among other things as the Truth. When we are truthful to the Word of God in obedience, we are girded with the belt of truth *(Eph. 6:4)*. The Word of God is a sword. We must know how to use this weapon not against our fellow believer or fellow man but against our adversary, the devil and his kingdom of darkness. Satan knows the Bible. He will distort the Word of God in an attempt to deceive. He quoted Scripture in his attempt to tempt Jesus Christ. We must use the weapon of the Word of God in a Christlike manner. The sword of the Spirit is the only armor listed in Ephesians 6 that is an offensive weapon. This sword belongs to the Spirit of God. In other words, it is not human words that defeat the devil. The sword of man has no power in spiritual warfare. In spiritual warfare, we need the sword of the Spirit.

> For the word of God is living and active. Sharper than any double-edged sword, it penetrates even to dividing soul and spirit, joints and marrow; it judges the thoughts and attitudes of the heart *(Heb. 4:12)*.

In Revelation 12, there was war in heaven and Satan was overcome by the blood of Christ and the word of testimony. In Matthew 4, when Satan confronted Christ to tempt him after a forty-day fast, Satan quoted Scripture. In response, Jesus dismissed Satan by quoting Scripture that revealed the deceptive motive of Satan. In this fight that we have been called to wage, we must know the Word of God and how to rightly handle it *(2 Tim.)*. In spiritual battle, you must stand on the Word of God and believe wholeheartedly in its truth.

When you do so, with the help of the Holy Spirit, it becomes a sword in your hand to overcome powers of darkness.

Prayer

> And pray in the Spirit on all occasions with all kinds of prayers and requests. With this in mind, be alert and always keep on praying for all the saints *(Eph. 6:18).*

We are called to be in persistent prayer always, especially as we stand against Satan and his schemes. We must imbibe the attitude of that persistent widow in Luke 18 who kept going to the unrighteous judge until she got victory (justice). There are so many things believers have to train themselves to pray about. If the majority of our prayer time with the Lord is centered on receiving material things, then we have not come into a maturity in the faith. As believers we need to pray for God's kingdom to come; we need to pray for the nations and the healing of the nations; we need to pray for a soul harvest in these end times; and we need to pray for the equipping of the saints all over the world, especially in areas where believers are experiencing severe persecution on account of their holding on to their faith in Christ. Our prayers in warfare must be geared at demolishing strongholds and everything that exalts itself against the knowledge of God. To effectively do this, we must learn to travail in prayer. Travailing prayer creates a deep burden and compelling passion to pray with intensity and violence. It is the kind of prayer accompanied by tongues, moaning, and groaning that words cannot utter. In this realm of travailing prayer, we gain the upper hand against satanic powers.

In this warfare, we need to take our prayers up into the heavenly realms to hinder the works of Satan over our communities and nations. We must pray for righteousness to be deposited into world systems and governments. Satan subtly uses governments and systems to spread his evil agenda across the world. This is why we must pray for our governments and for peace. In Jeremiah 29:7, God instructs the Israelites in exile to pray for their city of exile because if it prospers, they will prosper. Their prosperity was tied to that of their community. Our prayers must move from the confines of individualistic needs to addressing the needs of our communities and nations. Our prayers must be in the Spirit and are not to be done as a means to appease the flesh.

Luke 18:9–14:

> ⁹ To some who were confident of their own righteousness and looked down on everyone else, Jesus told this parable:
>
> ¹⁰ "Two men went up to the temple to pray, one a Pharisee and the other a tax collector.
>
> ¹¹ The Pharisee stood by himself and prayed: 'God, I thank you that I am not like other people—robbers, evildoers, adulterers—or even like this tax collector.
>
> ¹² I fast twice a week and give a tenth of all I get.'
>
> ¹³ "But the tax collector stood at a distance. He would not even look up to heaven, but beat his breast and said, 'God, have mercy on me, a sinner.'
>
> ¹⁴ "I tell you that this man, rather than the other, went home justified before God. For all those who exalt themselves will be humbled, and those who humble themselves will be exalted."

Even though the tax collector was a man despised by religious people, he humbled himself and asked for mercy. The Pharisee was foolish to measure himself against the tax collector and other men. The Pharisee put the tax collector down but God lifted him up. Effective prayer is not done by lifting ourselves up and putting others down. As a result of the tax collector showing humility and repentance in prayer,

God justified him. Prayer must be done in accordance with God's will. Prayer is instrumental to victory in any sphere of life. Through prayer we communicate with God and God communicates with us. Prayer enables us to live in righteousness. As we personalize and pray the Word we become more like the Word. A powerful way to use the Word of God is by personalizing and praying it.

> During the days of Jesus' life on earth, he offered up prayers and petitions with fervent cries and tears to the one who could save him from death, and he was heard because of his reverent submission *(Heb. 5:7)*.

To reiterate, Jesus was heard because of his reverent submission. We must be submitted to the Word of God for prayer to be meaningful. We must walk in righteousness. The effectual fervent prayer of a righteous man avails much *(James 5:16)*. Satan cannot stand against Word-based prayer because it is founded in absolute truth.

To intensify the reach and potency of our prayer, there is the need to fast. In the Bible, we see that whenever the people of God faced grave peril, they responded not only by praying to God but by fasting as well. Fasting requires that you deprive your body of its desires such as food, and if you are married, sex. Fasting suspends the legitimate demands of the body in order to build up the spirit as it seeks God to be more like Christ. Earlier on, we saw that the disciples were unable to cast out a particular demon because that type of demon could only be cast out through fasting and prayer. Fasting intensifies prayer by crucifying the flesh and making our spirits come alive.

Understanding Judges 20

Judges 20 gives us some insight into the mind of God in the course of warfare. The Israelites had to engage the tribe of Benjamin in a war. In Judges 20:18, the Israelites sought God's counsel in the war against Benjamin. They asked God which of the tribes of Israel should first attack Benjamin. This was somewhat presumptuous because they first should have asked God if they were to fight the tribe of Benjamin. God responded by saying that Judah should attack first. In spite of their relying on God's counsel, the Israelites lost the battle against the tribe of Benjamin. Why was this so? Well, unlike David, they did not ask the Lord if they were to go to battle. The right answer often begins with the right question. Pride made them assume victory and take it as a given.

In Judges 20:23, the Israelites sought God's counsel again concerning the war with Benjamin. This time they sought God's counsel with tears. Prior defeat made them now ask the right question, but they were still in the wrong position spiritually. They asked, "Shall I go up again to battle against the children of Benjamin my brother?" They asked the right question and got the right answer but the wrong result. God told Israel to go one more time against Benjamin, and one more time, Israel lost. Why was this so? The Israelites were again defeated by Benjamin in spite of their having the right answer because they were not in the right position spiritually. Seeking God with tears does not guarantee that you are right with God. Even Esau sought his blessing with tears, but tears were not sufficient to undo what had been done.

With two defeats against them, Israel now seeks God the right way and gets into the right position spiritually:

Then all the children of Israel, and all the people, went up, and came unto the house of God, and wept, and sat there before the Lord, and fasted that day until even, and offered burnt offerings and peace offerings before the Lord (Judg. 20:26).

After this, Israel got the victory in the war against the tribe of Benjamin. What did Israel do to overcome Benjamin that they had not done prior?

(i)   They sat before the Lord
(ii) Fasted, and
(iii) Presented offerings to God.

It was these three things that became the game changer in the war between Israel and Benjamin. As you fight spiritual warfare against powers of darkness, always inquire of the Lord in prayer. Do not offer presumptive and prideful prayers before the Lord. Seek in the Spirit what the game changers in the battle are and begin to employ them repeatedly against the enemy.

Faith

Another weapon we have against the enemy is our faith. Faith is a defensive and an offensive weapon. Ephesians 6:16 mentions the shield of faith. The shield of faith is a defensive armor.

> For whatsoever is born of God overcometh the world: and this is the victory that overcometh the world, even our faith *(1 John 4:4, KJV)*.

Faith has an overcoming power. Faith is the substance of things hoped for and the evidence of things not seen *(Heb. 11:1)*. If you hope for victory, you will need faith. If you are yet to see the victory, you will need faith to see it. This is what is implied in Hebrews 11:1. Generally speaking, Hebrews 11 encourages people of faith to persevere in trials, persecution, and warfare, and not to abandon their faith in times of difficulty. It is our ability and attitude of endurance in difficult times, especially when we are standing against the enemy's venomous attacks, that demonstrate our faith is real.

It is the shield of faith that protects us against the fiery darts of the wicked. It is our faith in the Word of God that enables us to stand against Satan and his fallen angels. Our strength is not based on what we may think or feel but on our faith in God's Word and promises. As you fight the good fight of faith, put all your trust in God.

Forsaking
All
I
Trust
Him

> Trust in the Lord with all your heart and lean not on your own understanding *(Prov. 3:5)*.

The Blood of Jesus

Another mighty weapon we use to engage and defeat powers of darkness is the blood of Jesus.

> Then he took the cup, gave thanks and offered it to them, saying, "Drink from it, all of you. This is my blood of the covenant, which is poured out for many for the forgiveness of sins" *(Matt. 26:27)*.

The blood of Jesus facilitates the forgiveness of sins. Without the shedding of blood, there can be no remission of sin *(Heb. 9:22)*. The blood of Jesus is sinless and so can take away sin. When we are cleansed from sin, the author of sin, Satan, has nothing in us *(John 14:30)*. The blood of Jesus removes sin and the condemnation that follows sin *(Heb. 10:14)*. One way to resist the spirit of condemnation is to hold on to Hebrews 10:24 and Romans 8:1–3. The blood of Jesus takes away sin. Sin must be dealt with because sin speaks. Sin accuses. The blood of Jesus silences the penalty and condemnation of sin.

Satan was defeated on the cross. The cross is the place where Jesus blood was shed. It is the place where Jesus was crucified to death.

> Blotting out the handwriting of ordinances that was against us, which was contrary to us, and took it out of the way, nailing it to his cross; and having spoiled principalities and powers, he made a shew of them openly, triumphing over them in it *(Col. 2:14–15, KJV)*.

Through the cross (death) of our Lord Jesus Christ, we have victory over Satan and his principalities and powers. This position is reinforced in Revelation 12:11: "And they overcame him (Satan) by the blood of the Lamb, and by the word of their testimony; and they loved not their lives unto the death."

Do not love your life to the extent that you are afraid of death. Do not entertain the devil's threats of death. Fight the good fight and you shall overcome in the name of Jesus. Take heed of God's advice given to Joshua: Be strong and very courageous. Meditate on the Word of God, and do not depart from obeying it.

Prayers for Engaging and Defeating Powers of Darkness

Meditate upon the following Scriptures: Ephesians 6:10–18; Luke 10:19; Matthew 11:12; Romans 8:31; 2 Corinthians 10:3–5; Colossians 2:14–15; and Revelation 12:7–11. Pray loud, boldly, and repeatedly until you see the victory:

1. I destroy and render powerless every household wickedness and familiar spirit by the consuming fire of God in Jesus' name.

2. In the name of Jesus, I dismantle, disorganize, and destroy every demonic network and satanic conspiracy against my life with the blood of Jesus.
3. In the name of Jesus, I trample upon and destroy every snake and scorpion and all the power of the enemy that has been opposing my destiny.
4. I destroy every family altar of witchcraft and remove myself from the jurisdiction of my family strong man in the mighty name of Jesus Christ.

6

DELIVERANCE FROM SEXUAL BONDAGE

Our world today and American society in particular is so fascinated and entrapped in a culture of sexual perversion and all manner of promiscuity. This sex-perverted culture does not even spare the children. The only sex that God approves is the sex within the confines of holy matrimony—marriage of one man and one wife to the exclusion of all others. Any sex outside of marriage is forbidden by God and carries with it drastic consequences, both spiritual and physical.

Sex establishes a blood covenant. Illicit sexual relationships and activities have grown at an alarming rate with equally frightening dimensions and intensity. The sexual revolution of the 1960s, which ushered in an open sex culture, has not only changed society, it has adversely changed our churches. It is becoming more difficult to tell if differences exist between the sexual conduct of Christians and that of non-Christians. A disturbing trend is that many Christians have carried over their thought patterns when they were unbelievers. Their embracing of the Christian faith has not challenged them to question their sexual behaviors. They have not metamorphosed into that new creation in Christ and are still holding on to the old things *(2 Cor. 5:17)*.

Dearly beloved, I beseech you as strangers and pilgrims, abstain from fleshly lusts, which war against the soul *(1 Pet. 2:11, KJV)*.

But put ye on the Lord Jesus Christ, and make not provision for the flesh, to fulfil the lusts thereof *(Rom. 13:14, KJV)*.

Flee also youthful lusts: but follow righteousness, faith, charity, peace, with them that call on the Lord out of a pure heart *(2 Tim. 2:22, KJV)*.

The above-mentioned Scripture verses command us to flee and abstain from lust by not making provision for the flesh to be in control. If you make accommodation for your flesh, you will fulfill the lusts thereof. In examining the stronghold of sexual sin and how to overcome it, we must understand how our fleshly carnal desires generate a lust that craves to be satisfied in disregard of the Word of God. The Bible tells us to flee lust. Joseph was attacked by lust in Genesis 39:6–12, and he fled, leaving his garment behind for Potiphar's wife. You must even run faster than Joseph did because the longer you linger around lust, the more vulnerable you become. To overcome lust, crucify the flesh and flee lust. Do not put yourself in a position where you will have to rely on your flesh, because your flesh will fail you. Until we understand how to deal with lust, we will not get deliverance from sexual bondage.

Lust

In Galatians 5:16–17, KJV, we are instructed to live by the Spirit so that we do not gratify the desires of the sinful nature:

This I say then, Walk in the Spirit, and ye shall not fulfil the lusts of the flesh. For the flesh lusteth against the Spirit, and the Spirit against the flesh: and these are contrary the one to the other: so that ye cannot do the things that ye would.

The Bible makes it clear that the only way not to yield to lust is to walk in the Spirit. The Spirit is contrary to the flesh and lust flows from our fallen, corrupt, and sinful condition (the flesh). Walking in the Spirit demands abiding by the Word of God and crucifying the flesh so that it cannot even make a case to be heard. If the flesh is not crucified to death, it will continue working. The only way to prevent the flesh from working is to crucify it by walking in the Spirit. Galatians 5:19–21, KJV, below, lists the works of the flesh. These are things the flesh can drive us to be consumed in against our will if we are not walking and living in the Spirit.

> [19] Now the works of the flesh are manifest, which are these; Adultery, fornication, uncleanness, lasciviousness,
> [20] Idolatry, witchcraft, hatred, variance, emulations, wrath, strife, seditions, heresies,
> [21] Envyings, murders, drunkenness, revellings, and such like: of the which I tell you before, as I have also told you in time past, that they which do such things shall not inherit the kingdom of God.

The Spirit and the flesh are at war with each other in the life of the believer. The Bible lists some of the works of the flesh as sins of sexual immorality, such as adultery, fornication, and lasciviousness. It is worthy to note that these sins are listed as the works of the flesh and not the works of the devil. The devil gains entrance into lives through lust. A spirit of lust is fed by the flesh and so that spirit of lust will dive into the flesh to carry out its carnal desires. When the flesh is not crucified, it becomes the devil's playground. The goal of the flesh is to have control in the believer's life so that it can begin to express itself in lust. Until the flesh and its lusts are dealt with, believers will record little or no success with their desire, if at all, to be delivered from sexual immorality.

Lust is an extension of the flesh. Your flesh is the outer man. Your spirit is the inner man. God resides in the inner man. The inner man is saved. The outer man is not. The outer man is not going to heaven. Flesh and blood cannot inherit the kingdom of God *(1 Cor. 15:50)*. God is very clear when it comes to lust. Lust results in death. God planned it so that the inner man will control and dominate the outer man. Your inner man is called by God to supervise the outer man, but when we walk in the flesh, the outer man supervises the inner man. All the outer man knows is lust. Lust is not limited to sexual lust. Lust is any carnal desire that God does not approve of.

> For I know that in me (that is, in my flesh,) dwelleth no good thing: for to will is present with me; but how to perform that which is good I find not *(Rom. 7:18, KJV)*.

In Romans 7:18, Apostle Paul says that in his flesh (the outer man) there is nothing good but in his inner man he wills to do the good. However, he is unable to do so. When this is the case, it is always because the outward man is exercising control over the inward man. The outward man wants to commit sexual sins and other sins and will do so if not restrained and crucified by the inward man. Romans 7 presents a real picture before us: that it is possible to love God so much and so sincerely in the inner man and yet sin so frequently and casually against God in the outer man *(Rom. 7:20–22)*. This is why we struggle with sin, including sexual sin, because two men are living inside us. One of them has to die. The old man (the outer man) has to die so that the new man (inner man) can express itself to the glory of God.

The inner man is the one that is saved. We need deliverance from the outer man. It is the outer man that invites demons into believers' lives. It is the outer man that keeps believers bound in addictions. Satan knows that the only way he can subject us to his control and oppression is through our outer man, and so he will do everything to resurrect the outer man. Satan seeks to raise up the outer man so that it can fight and frustrate the inner man.

> I thank God through Jesus Christ our Lord. So then with the mind I myself serve the law of God; but with the flesh the law of sin *(Rom. 7:25, KJV)*.

In Romans 7:25, Paul is saying that with his mind (inner man, new man, his spirit), he serves God, but with his flesh (the outer man, old man), he serves sin. This is why the flesh must be crucified. If the flesh is not crucified, you will serve the law of sin. The flesh—the carnal mind—is hostile to God and cannot please God *(Rom. 8:6–7)*. Romans 8:13 carries a severe warning for believers. Paul's letter is written to the saints in Rome and in Romans 8, he warns the believers in Rome about the consequences of pleasing their flesh: "For if ye live after the flesh, ye shall die: but if ye through the Spirit do mortify the deeds of the body, ye shall live" *(Rom. 8:13)*. As a believer, do not believe the lie that you can live a lifestyle of sin and still go to heaven. For without holiness no one will see God *(Heb. 12:14)*. The Bible tells us those that truly belong to Jesus Christ are not those that merely come to the church altars and say a sinner's prayer. They are not those that merely talk Christian language to impress others. The Bible makes it clear who those that truly belong to Jesus Christ are:

> Those who belong to Christ Jesus have crucified the sinful nature with its passions and desires *(Gal. 5:24)*.

There is therefore now no condemnation to them which are in Christ Jesus, who walk not after the flesh, but after the Spirit *(Rom. 8:1, KJV)*.

Simply put, those that belong to Christ take seriously working on the need to keep their flesh crucified and their inner man renewed. They do so by walking after the Spirit.

Closely related to the lust of the flesh is the lust of the eyes *(1 John 2:16)*. The lust of the eyes helps feed the lust of the flesh. The lust of the eyes, oftentimes, is the gate to the lust of the flesh. The lust of the eyes is the craving to see what God has forbidden man to see. It is the craving to see that which eventually ends up contaminating the human soul with memories that cannot be so easily erased. The lust of the eyes always comes through visual appeal. When Satan tempted Eve in the Garden of Eden, Eve succumbed when she saw that the fruit of the tree was good for food and pleasing to the eye (visual appeal) *(Gen. 3:6)*. When Satan sought to tempt Jesus in Matthew 4, he showed him (visual appeal) all the kingdoms of the world and their splendor *(Matt. 4:8)*. We must guard our eye gates so that lust does not enter into and infiltrate our hearts.

I made a covenant with my eyes not to look lustfully at a girl *(Job 31:1)*.

If like Job we do not make a covenant with our eyes, we will begin to look lustfully at the opposite sex. Today, we need to make that covenant not to feed our eyes on garbage such as pornography and the opposite sex dressed half-naked on our streets. The lust of the eyes is what has bound many Christians into pornography. Satan has been merciless and quick in keeping these Christians addicted to pornography. Many have viewed it hoping to do so only once to satisfy the lust of their eyes, but to their frustration and disgust, they have been unable to break away from this because it has them bound. It has them bound and addicted because it is a spirit. Jesus said that if your eye causes you to sin, pluck it out. To be clear, if your eye causes you to lust, close them when the temptation comes. Don't just turn your head away; close your eyes if safety permits.

Satan uses temptation to stir up lusts. Lust gives temptation the right to become sin. Many Christians who are in sexual immorality and want a way out must fight the battle first at the moment of temptation.

> Let no man say when he is tempted, I am tempted of God: for God cannot be tempted with evil, neither tempteth he any man: But every man is tempted, when he is drawn away of his own lust, and enticed. Then when lusteth conceived, it bringeth forth sin: and sin, when it is finished, bringeth forth death *(James 1:13–16, KJV)*.

So long as we have this flesh, lust is present. What you do with your flesh will determine what happens to your lust and whether you are enticed and driven to commit sexual sins. We must crucify the flesh and walk in the Spirit. If we do not crucify the flesh, the flesh will eventually drive us to do its work mentioned in Galatians 5:19–21.

Sexual Sins

As we have seen from portions of Scripture, the main key to deliverance from sexual bondage is overcoming lust by walking in the Spirit. Lust is very deceptive and translates into fantasy, imaginations, and impure thoughts. You must cast down imaginations and every high thing that exalts itself against the knowledge of God and bring into captivity every thought to the obedience of Christ. Thoughts and imaginations are powerful and equally as culpable as acts. Prior to Christ, men thought of sexual sins as being limited to sexual acts.

1. Adultery and Fornication

You have heard that it was said, 'Do not commit adultery.' But I tell you that anyone who looks at a woman lustfully has already committed adultery with her in his heart *(Matt. 5:27–28)*.

Many believers have not committed the physical act of adultery, but as far as God is concerned, they are adulterers because the evil transaction is taking place in their heart. The Word of God tells us to flee fornication. The Bible does not tell us to resist fornication like it tells us to resist Satan when submitted to God. James 4:7 tells us to submit ourselves to God and to resist the devil, and the devil will flee. We do not flee from the devil: we resist him and he flees from us. As strong as Satan may be, we are not instructed to flee from him. Rather, we are instructed to flee fornication *(1 Cor. 6:18)*. Fornication is participating in premarital sex and sex between unmarried persons. Adultery is sex between a married person with someone other than his or her spouse.

2. Pornography. Pornography could express itself in video, still photography, drawings, sculpture, and artistic works, audio, music lyrics, and literature of a sexually explicit nature. Pornography is not, as many think, a victimless crime. It works on the human imagination and provokes it to commit fornication via fantasy. Pornography grew with the advent of the Internet, which fueled the expansion of its reach to all age groups. Pornography breeds sexual lusts and draws its victims to other sexual sins like masturbation, rape, and incest, because it is a spirit accompanied by other related spirits. The spirit of pornography demands that its victims crave for more. Pornography is addictive and arouses sexual passions and desires to the extent that people look for sexual satisfaction outside of marriage. Pornography is a spirit that has been responsible for opening the door to other spirits of sexual perversion that have worked to destroy many marriages.

3. Perverted Sex. The wickedness of man has succeeded in perverting sex both within and outside the confines of marriage. Perverted sex comes in various forms.

Masturbation is an act of self-stimulation of the sexual organs to achieve orgasm without sexual intercourse. This is selfish sex whereby the perpetrator becomes both the man and the woman at the same time. In masturbation, the person masturbating is having an affair with himself or herself. The Bible is somewhat silent on the issue of masturbation. Like pornography and other sexual sins, masturbation becomes addictive because the practice opens the door for sexual demons to come in and make the perpetrator a slave to it by demanding more and more. This results in sexual bondage because the person may try to stop the habit of masturbation and find out that he or she cannot. This is almost always the case because a bigger invincible power (a demon) is now entrenched in this habit-forming exercise. This demon will override the person's determination to stop, and deliverance will be required to set the person free. In recent times, there has been an increase in medical literature endorsing masturbation as having health benefits. These so-called health benefits, whether proven or not, do not address the demonic enslavement of its perpetrator-victims. Let God be true and every man a liar.

Another form of perverted sex is oral sex. *Chambers Dictionary* defines oral sex as sexual relations involving the use of the mouth to stimulate the genitals of one's partner. Oral sex is a spirit that perverts the true method of sex.

Homosexuality and lesbianism are other forms of perverted sex that are firmly entrenched by very powerful sexual demons. Deliverance in this area has proven to be more intense as these demonic powers are so determined to keep their victims enslaved in same-sex relationships.

Do not lie with a man as one lies with a woman; that is detestable *(Lev. 18:22)*.

Romans 1:24–28:

²⁴Therefore God gave them over in the sinful desires of their hearts to sexual impurity for the degrading of their bodies with one another.
²⁵ They exchanged the truth about God for a lie, and worshiped and served created things rather than the Creator—who is forever praised. Amen.
²⁶ Because of this, God gave them over to shameful lusts. Even their women exchanged natural sexual relations for unnatural ones.
²⁷ In the same way the men also abandoned natural relations with women and were inflamed with lust for one another. Men committed shameful acts with other men, and received in themselves the due penalty for their error.
²⁸ Furthermore, just as they did not think it worthwhile to retain the knowledge of God, so God gave them over to a depraved mind, so that they do what ought not to be done.

To complicate matters, those bound by homosexuality and lesbianism have been given over to a depraved, reprobate mind by God Himself. Deliverance here must work in restoring the reprobate mind through deep repentance in addition to casting out the demons involved.

Illicit Sexual Partners

In the cast of several illicit sexual partners, we shall briefly examine three types of illicit sexual partners:

1. The Prostitute
2. The Rapist
3. Incubus and Succubus

The Prostitute

For a prostitute is a deep pit and a wayward wife is a narrow well. Like a bandit she lies in wait, and multiplies the unfaithful among men *(Prov. 23:27–28).*

A man who loves wisdom brings joy to his father, but a companion of prostitutes squanders his wealth *(Prov. 29:3).*

Do you not know that he who unites himself with a prostitute is one with her in body? For it is said, "The two will become one flesh" *(1 Cor. 6:16).*

Having a prostitute as a past or current sexual partner carries a lot of dangers. Prostitution involves the exchange of money or favors for sex. The Bible calls a prostitute a deep pit. Inside a deep pit is so much garbage. A prostitute is a container that houses numerous demons. She has invested in the demons of her uncountable sex partners and becomes a clearinghouse for receiving and exchanging demons of all kinds. To make matters worse, when a person has sex with a prostitute he becomes one with her. That means that the prostitute shares all that she has with him in exchange for his money. His money is buying more than what he bargained for, including the risk of disease and loss of reputation. The prostitute gives her client some demons, and immediately those demons begin to work on destroying that client's life. In the parable of the prodigal son, the older brother accuses his father of showing mercy and favor to the younger brother that squandered his wealth on prostitutes *(Luke 15:30)*. A prostitute is a deep pit. Many men have lost their virtues and their destinies in this deep pit.

Prostitution is sex without any commitment. It is just a contract for sinful services. Yet this is the ultimate lie because sex is not just physical, it is spiritual. Sexual immorality is a sin that affects not only the body but the spirit *(1 Cor. 18–20)*. Prostitution, in particular, has the propensity to be spiritually fatal because it creates multiple soul ties with multiple strangers, thereby fragmenting the soul to bits and pieces.

The Rapist

In prostitution there is consent with the consideration of a fee for sex. With rape, there is no consent. One person is violated by another. In the restrictive sense, rape is the unlawful, nonconsensual act of a man using his penis to penetrate a woman's vagina. The rapist could be a total stranger or a known person to the woman. In any case, the woman is sexually violated against her will and has now been joined with a man that is not of her choosing. Now, part of that man is living in her. She will need inner healing and deliverance not only from sexual spirits but from spirits of trauma as well. Rape is a crime of violence and very often, violent spirits are the ones that define the agenda of rape. Sexual sins are all interconnected. For example, pornography arouses lust, and people look for outlets to release the sexual tension that it creates, only for them to realize that it creates a cycle of sexual tension that is never satisfied and, as such, always demands more release. The rapist has never thought of crucifying his flesh.

For a woman, the vagina is the gate to her womb. As a woman, you must be very careful who enters through the gate because he usually is not coming alone. He is coming not only with his DNA but with spirits that may be in him. Your gate was made to permit entry to only one Adam, the man that God has ordained for you. Every other man is a trespasser carrying burdens you were not created to share with him. As a woman, be strong, be wise. Do not just allow anyone to deposit their seed in you. It could be poisonous seed. Test the spirit of the man to know who and what you are inviting into your life. Certain things come with ease but are very difficult to drive out.

Incubus and Succubus

The incubus spirit is a demon in male form that sexually attacks women. The counterpart spirit that attacks men is the succubus spirit. In some deliverance parlances, these may be described as spirit husbands, spirit wives, or spirit spouses. They are referred to as spouses when there is a hidden covenant in the spirit realm that gives the demon some legal right to have a marital relationship with a human being. This concept is not alien to the Bible.

> There were giants in the earth in those days; and also after that, when the sons of God came in unto the daughters of men, and they bare children to them, the same became mighty men which were of old, men of renown *(Gen. 6:4)*.

There is some controversy regarding the actual identity of the sons of God in Genesis 6:4. The Scripture is clear that the daughters were of humanity. But the sons are described with a character of divinity. In Genesis 6:4, sons of God had sex with daughters of men and begat children. They were all destroyed in the deluge of Genesis 7. In Job 1:6, the term "sons of God" is descriptive of angelic beings: "Now there was a day when the sons of God came to present themselves before the Lord, and Satan came also among them." Most likely, in Genesis 6:4, sons of God is a reference to angelic beings. Angelic beings are spirits. These spirits entered into women and begat children. Today, these spirits are still harassing the daughters of man and violating their sexuality. The incubus and succubus spirits fight to have a sexual intimacy with their victim. People have testified of feeling hands touching and fondling them without seeing anyone and then all of a sudden they have reached orgasm. They know when the demonic presence is around them through its certain manifestations. Others have sex in their dreams continually with the same spirit being.

In the course of a deliverance and prayer session for Sister August, she told us that she felt hands slapping her forehead at night in retaliation for her wanting to be free from demons. As we worked on her deliverance in the name of Jesus, the demon in question burst out saying, "Yes, I am the one that slaps her on the head because she is very stubborn." Our place is not to interrogate demons, but I asked the demon why he did that and it said that anytime he slapped her forehead, she would be confused and disoriented and never do well at her job interviews. We bound that particular demon in the name of Jesus and cast it out. Within a month, Sister August got a good job and is still gainfully employed. If a spirit can slap someone on the forehead, it will have no problem fondling that person's sexual organs unless by covenant it has yielded that right to another evil spirit.

We have also witnessed instances where in the course of deliverance, an incubus demon has manifested and began to have sexual intercourse with the woman being delivered. We bound that wicked spirit, but before it was bound we were able to see the woman moving in response to invisible sexual activity. Trained deliverance workers covered the woman's midsection to maintain her dignity. By the manifestation, we knew what kind of demon we were dealing with.

In the spirit realm, particularly in some African societies, babies are dedicated to familiar spirits through a Covenant of Dedication, which gives these familiar spirits a legal right to be joined with these babies for life. These familiar spirits, through a covenant, are married to family members for the duration of their lives and play a major role in affecting their destiny. Some incubus and succubus spirits bring wealth to their human partners while others bring poverty and torment. Because these demons view themselves as being one (through the act of sexual intercourse) with the daughters and sons of men, they hold on to the right to withhold blessings that belong to their human victims. In the spirit realm, when a blessing is to be released, a spirit spouse can intercept and confiscate it on the basis of "what belongs to my spouse belongs to me." This demon can be so brazen because a soul tie has been created between it and its victim; they are one flesh until a separation is made through prayer and deliverance.

Permit me to reproduce a correspondence I received verbatim in my Facebook email account on March 16, 2014. The only thing I have not reproduced is the identity of the person, whom I will call "Miss July." I also had to redact some sexually expletive words with the symbol "--".

> Miss July: Hi pastor ID. I would like to ask you a question before doing something. There is a voodoo master who said to me that if I have sex with him for 7 days and 7 nights I will have all that I want in this world, fame, money all that I want (He said that is not him who is asking me do to that but Satan himself). I know you were involved in the occult, so please tell me what the 7 days and 7 nights mean in the spiritual world? I know he is possessed with thousands of demons. Could I be killed by having sex with him and being possessed by hundreds of demons at once? Thank you.

> Pastor ID: Why would you even entertain such a thought? What does it profit a man to gain the world

and lose his soul? Just by talking to this man, you are already tangoing with demons. Ask God to cleanse you with the blood of His Son, Jesus Christ from all this contamination through contact with an occult master. I am sorry, but I don't see of what use my sharing my thoughts on what 7 days and 7 nights could mean will help matters. Stay clear of danger. Be wise.

Miss July: I didn't ask you to preach for me you idiot. I asked you a f--king question, f--k off you are useless!!

At this point, I did not bother continuing the conversation because I knew the demons were talking through her. So here is a woman wanting to sleep with an occult priest carrying thousands of demons just for the sake of earthly riches that do not endure. A man who sleeps with such a woman in the future will be in for very big trouble with satanic powers.

Consequences of Sexual Sin

This is a point where one has to be blunt and call a spade a spade. The Bible makes it clear that those who practice fornication will end up in hell. If you are sexually immoral, you will end up in hellfire! Do not be fooled by the devil telling you that you are born again and yet you have not yet repented *(Rev. 21:8)*. That is a false salvation. It is by your fruit that heaven knows you. You are not saved by works, but works tell us whether one is truly saved. The consequences of sexual immorality are spiritual and physical.

Judges Chapters 13–16

Samson was a strong man. He allowed a woman of questionable character, a strange woman called Delilah, to cut off his hair and by implication, his strength. Many men of God have had their hair shaved off by the Delilahs of this world, and as a result their eyes have been gouged out by demons, just like Samson experienced owing to his carelessness and carnality. Many have lost their effectiveness in Christ because of sexual sin. Samson the mighty was brought to zero by his insatiable appetite for sex outside the boundaries that God had set.

The visible consequences of sexual sins in our generation have included the spread of sexually transmitted diseases like AIDS and HIV, herpes and chlamydia; loss of reproductive capacities in males and females through STDs; an increase in unwanted pregnancies in spite of various new forms of contraception; abortions; increase in sexual abuse and rapes; divorces and separation of married couples; and sex scandals among Christian and secular leaders. Sexual demons are on the loose to magnify and expand these consequences by working hard to ensure that man does not crucify his flesh and walk in the Spirit.

Deliverance is seriously and urgently needed in this area, but unfortunately the laborers that know what to do are few and are often overstretched and fatigued from being in deliverance's combative warfare for long periods of time. Those that are trapped in sexual bondage must be very determined and desperate to break loose from every habit-forming practice; they must be desperate and determined to fight and cast out every evil spirit working within and without to keep them bound perpetually in sexual immorality. To be free, you must be willing and determined to be free. If the Son sets you free you will be free indeed *(John 8:36)*. This is the truth for getting deliverance in this difficult area. By holding on to the teaching of Jesus Christ, you will know the truth and the truth will set you free *(John 8:32)*.

Prayers for Release from Powers of Sexual Perversion

Meditate on Psalm 51; Romans 1:18–32; Romans 6:12–14; 1 Corinthians 3:16–17; and 2 Corinthians 6:14–18. Pray these prayers out loud with conviction, faith, and authority:

1. I confess and declare that my body is a temple of the Holy Spirit, redeemed and cleansed by the blood of Jesus. Therefore, I command in the name of Jesus, every spirit of lust and sexual perversion defiling me to be bound and cast out in the name of Jesus.

2. In the name of Jesus, I confess and repent of all my sexual sins and ask you Lord Jesus to forgive me of these sins and sanctify me body, soul, and spirit with your blood.

3. In the name of Jesus, I surrender all my body parts, including my sexual organs to the righteousness of God in Christ Jesus and forbid powers of darkness from using any part of my body or my mind for evil sexual purposes.

4. In the name of Jesus and by the power in the blood of Jesus, I break every evil soul tie I have with past sexual partners through sexual sin.

5. By my act of confession, repentance, and receiving forgiveness, I command in the name of Jesus that every spirit of lust and sexual perversion in my life be bound and cast out.

6. In the name of Jesus, I ask that the consuming fire of the Holy Spirit enter into me and burn to ashes every unholy appetite and desire for illicit sexual activity.

7. In the name of Jesus, I recover my virtues, my semen, my body fluids, my perspiration, and my panting and moaning from every satanic bank and satanic altar and forbid them to be used against me in the name of Jesus.

8. In the name of Jesus Christ, let the fire of God enter into me and destroy every evil deposit that the enemy placed in me as a result of my past sexual sin.

9. In the name of Jesus, I reject every sexual dream and every being that attempts to or that has had sex with

me in the dream. I break every soul tie with incubus and succubus in the mighty name of Jesus.

10. In the name of Jesus and by the power in the blood of Jesus, I break every covenant with a spirit spouse and refuse to be bound by evil spiritual covenants.

11. I break the power and hold every spirit of pornography and masturbation has over me in the name of Jesus Christ. With the help of the Holy Spirit and in the name of Jesus Christ, I refuse to obey the evil suggestions and commands of the spirits of masturbation and pornography.

12. I renounce, in the name of Jesus, every covenant I made apart from God that ties me to a being that is unwilling to let go. Let the fire of God scatter unto desolation every power that has vowed to keep me a slave to sexual sin in the mighty name of Jesus Christ.

7

Deliverance and Healing of Marriages

Many couples enter into marriage with high realistic hopes and good intentions only to be confronted by the wiles of the devil. Some others stumble into marriage without really thinking it through and seeking the will of God in prayer. After a while, the devil will make one spouse think that the other spouse is the enemy. Your spouse is not your enemy, and you must never view a spouse as an enemy. When there is tension in the marriage, it is prudent to check who really is pulling the strings. We wrestle not against flesh and blood. Satan hates the Christian marriage. Satan is the god of this world *(2 Cor. 4:4)*, and he is influencing society to erode and devalue the institution of marriage. Satan has no element of love in him, and so he does all he can to destroy marriage. God is Love and the foundation of marriage is Love. Love in a stable Christian home prepares the children of such homes from childhood through adolescence to have healthy marriages. Train up a child in the way he should go: and when he is old, he will not depart from it *(Prov. 22:6)*. Many children are growing up in broken homes and have no example of a healthy Christian marriage before them to train them on how to have a healthy marriage when they become adults.

A Christian marriage is the voluntary union of one man and one woman in covenant to the exclusion of all others for life. Same-sex marriages, even though now allowed by US law all across the land, are not biblical and are not Christian marriages.

> Then the Lord God made a woman from the rib he had taken out of the man, and he brought her to the man. The man said, "This is now bone of my bones and flesh of my flesh; she shall be called 'woman,' for she was taken out of man." For this reason a man will leave his father and mother and be united to his wife, and they will become one flesh *(Gen. 2:22–24)*.

> Some Pharisees came to him to test him. They asked, "Is it lawful for a man to divorce his wife for any and every reason?" "Haven't you read," he replied, "that at the beginning the Creator 'made them male and female,' and said, 'For this reason a man will leave his father and mother and be united to his wife, and the two will become one flesh'? So they are no longer two, but one. Therefore what God has joined together, let man not separate" *(Matt. 19:3–6)*.

From the outset, Satan will try to get us to be unequally yoked in our marriages so that we start on a weak foundation and he has the advantage over us. It is for this reason that God strongly warns us not to be unequally yoked:

> Do not be yoked together with unbelievers. For what do righteousness and wickedness have in common? Or what fellowship can light have with darkness? What harmony is there between Christ and Belial? What

does a believer have in common with an unbeliever? *(2 Cor. 6:14–15).*

Do not intermarry with them. Do not give your daughters to their sons or take their daughters for your sons, for they will turn your sons away from following me to serve other gods, and the Lord's anger will burn against you and will quickly destroy you *(Deut. 7:3–4).*

Do not plow with an ox and a donkey yoked together *(Deut. 22:10).*

In Ephesians 5, the mystery of marriage is discussed and we see that God ordained marriage on earth to reflect the relationship between Christ and the Church. There are no marriages in heaven, save the marriage in Revelation 19 between Christ and the Church. On earth, God ordained marriage for His glory. This is the plan of God for Christian marriages, but Satan comes to steal, to kill, and to destroy. Satan is the architect of misunderstanding and conflict in our homes. He knows that if he can destroy a marriage, he has destroyed the home. Satan will fight against our determination to remain in our marriages, and we must submit to God and resist him. If you are ignorant of the devil's devices, it will be very hard for you to stay in your marriage or to enjoy it. The problem with many marriages lies in the manner in which they were entered into. When Christians enter into marriage unequally yoked or without seeking the will of God, the marriage starts off on a shaky foundation and opens doors for demons. Some have married on the basis of outward beauty instead of inward character. What use is a spouse with outward beauty who is deficient in character? A deficient character walks in the flesh and is a conducive entry point for all manner of demonic infestation.

At times, marriage is like a heavy cross, and this is why the vows of holy matrimony emphasize "for better or for worse."

Marriage could be a very heavy cross to bear. The cross of Christ was heavy and yet Christ did not shrink back from the burden of his cross. In marriage, two imperfect people are being joined together, and this could be quite a heavy burden. Christ could have shrunk back from the cross but He chose to carry it for our sake and for the love He had for us and the Father. This same kind of agape love is what must be used to secure marriages against the onslaught of Satan and his demons. Of course, we must also be mindful not to live in the flesh but to walk in the Spirit.

A visible and an invisible war are being executed against Christian marriages. Known Satanists have been reported to confess how they have fasted and are fasting against Christian homes and marriages. Christian marriages are under increasing attack, and we must know how to fight back and recover marriages under the influence and control of powers of darkness.

The Bible says in Amos 3:3, "Can two walk together except they be agreed?" For Christian marriages to be strong, spouses must learn to agree with each other. It takes two people to disagree, but it only takes one person to agree. If need be, each spouse must be determined to be that one person who agrees. For example, even though Christ was in the right, He chose to agree with the cross. If Christ chose to appeal against the verdict of the cross, He would have been justified, but yet, Christ chose to agree with the cross. The Mightier One agreed with the lesser one so that the will and plan of God since creation may be accomplished. In our Christian walk, we will be called to displease ourselves in order to please our spouses. This is agape love—sacrificial love. Ephesians 5:21 enjoins us to submit ourselves one to another in the fear of God. We do not submit because we are right. We submit because we fear God and want to please Him. Ephesians 5:22 calls on wives to submit to their husbands as unto the Lord, and Ephesians

5:25 calls on husbands to love their wives even as Christ also loved the Church and gave Himself for her.

> Wives, submit to your husbands, as is fitting in the Lord. Husbands, love your wives and do not be harsh with them *(Col. 3:18–19)*.

The Jezebel spirit propels many women to push for control in their homes and marriages. The influence of Jezebel encourages the wife to be assertive and to seek to dominate and be in charge. God gave this authority (which comes from the responsibility of agape love) to the man. Jezebel had no authority of her own—she usurped King Ahab's authority in order to carry out her sinister objectives.

Each spouse in a marriage is responsible for building a strong, healthy marriage. We must be determined to be that spouse regardless of our partner's actions, and as we do so, we will begin to progressively limit the activities of satanic powers in our homes and marriages. Conflicts are inevitable in relationships, and the question becomes how we respond to and resolve them. Demons like to capitalize on marital conflicts and turn them into instruments for the very destruction of marriages. We must be willing to resolve conflicts quickly, in love and in humility. When a husband and wife have a quarrel, the world teaches us that the wrong spouse should apologize. Actually, as Christians, we are made to understand that it is the spouse who loves the most that will apologize first. Resolving marital conflicts often has little to do with who is right and who is wrong. Pursuing that course often leads to more accusations and bitterness. The one who loves the most is the one who will apologize whether right or wrong.

A Word for the Woman

In *Be God's Gift to Your Husband*, Dr. Adesuwa Anwuri advises the woman thus:

Be your husband's encourager . . . Be the biblical help-mate. A helper is someone who is useful to somebody. A helper is not the main actor but should be strong enough to be of help . . . she should be a contributor. She should appreciate and realize that her husband is the final authority in the home. "I do not permit a woman to have authority over a man . . . 1 Timothy 2:12." A wife is to help her husband fulfil the call of God on his life.

A woman must not use her marriage as a launching pad to further her own personal agenda. She is called to be a helpmate.

Submission is a key to accomplish God's purpose. Submission is one of the most difficult actions a wife will have to undertake, and she can only do so with the grace and power of God. Jesus submitted to the Father in order to accomplish salvation. He did not question whether that was fair. A husband is God's delegated authority over his wife, and the devil does all he can to abuse and usurp that authority. Wives, please avoid the temptation of usurping your husband's authority. David's wife, Michal, accused David of behaving shamelessly, and her marriage to her husband became a barren marriage *(2 Sam. 6:20–23)*.

- Jezebel usurped King Ahab's authority
- Queen Vashti was disobedient to her husband, King Artaxerxes, and so she lost her position.
- Queen Esther, on the contrary, was obedient to her elder cousin, Mordecai (authority figure), and subsequently to King Artaxerxes, and she rose in influence.

Wives have a good godly example in Queen Esther. A wife must reject the spirit of Vashti, which refuses to submit to God-given authority because of his imperfections.

A Word for the Man

God ordained men to be head over their families, and God has expectations concerning the position of authority He has placed upon man.

First, as the head, man must take his example from Christ:

> "But I would have you know, that the head of every man is Christ; and the head of the woman is the man; and the head of Christ is God" *(1 Cor. 11:3)*.

> Even as the Son of man came not to be ministered unto but to minister, and to give His life as a ransom for many *(Matt. 20:28)*.

To strengthen their marriages and keep the enemy out, men must learn to wash the feet of their wives even when their wives kick them with those feet. As the head, the man becomes the servant. Stewardship demands that husbands wash the feet of their wives and children without even expecting them to do the same. The divine order for the home is Christ as the ultimate head with the husband's headship, wife's submission, and children's obedience. In this manner, the rule of Christ is demonstrated in the home.

Second, men must love their wives *(Eph. 5:22)* regardless of their behavior.

1 Corinthians 13:4–8:

> [4] Love is patient, love is kind. It does not envy, it does not boast, it is not proud.
> [5] It does not dishonor others, it is not self-seeking, it is not easily angered, it keeps no record of wrongs.
> [6] Love does not delight in evil but rejoices with the truth.
> [7] It always protects, always trusts, always hopes, always perseveres.

[8] Love never fails. But where there are prophecies, they will cease; where there are tongues, they will be stilled; where there is knowledge, it will pass away.

We see the description of true love here in 1 Corinthians 13:4–8. Agape love gives and protects in spite of the absence of reciprocity.

Third, in the husband's priesthood capacity as priest of the home *(1 Cor. 11:3)*, he is required to intercede for his home—his wife and his children.

Keeping the Devil Out of Our Marriages and the Healing of Our Marriages

What we have been discussing so far is what couples must do to strengthen their marriages and create a godly atmosphere for their marriage to grow. It is so important for a marriage to be built on a strong foundation so that when the storms of life challenge it, it will stand. There is a war against marriage that has been unleashed, and it is being fought in the spirit realm with visible earthly manifestations and consequences: divorce, same-sex marriage, adultery, domestic violence, child abuse, shacking up without commitment, etc. Satan, in his hatred for marriages, is determined to spoil and break them. We are entreated by 2 Corinthians 2:11 not to be ignorant of Satan's devices so that Satan does not take advantage over us.

The Word of God encourages the people of God to marry and increase *(Jer. 29:5–6)*. Proverbs 18:22 says that he who finds a wife finds what is good and receives favor from the Lord. Hebrews 13:4 demands that marriage should be honored by all, and the marriage bed kept pure, for God will judge the adulterer and all the sexually immoral. Matthew 19:6 states that husband and wife are no longer two, but one, and that therefore, what God has joined together, let no man separate. These Scriptures demonstrate that it is God who ordained marriage. Hence, God's enemies seek to pollute marriage and bring it into disrepute. In their war against marriage, the kingdom of darkness is adept at planting strongholds in the carnal minds of believers. To have strong and healthy marriages, we must keep the following things, among other harmful things, out of our lives: pride, anger, accusations, suspicions, strife, lack of communication and miscommunication, insecurities, fear, domination and control, unforgiveness, ungodly soul ties, selfishness, sexual perversion, lack of trust, lack of submission, etc. These things are very toxic to a marriage, and Satan seeks to feed them into a marriage in large doses.

A little leaven leaveneth the whole lump *(Gal. 5:9)*.

Issues in marriage may start off as little things and grow uncontrollably. It is the little foxes that spoil the vine *(Song of Sol. 2:15)*. Some little character flaw often spoils the vine: the marriage relationship. We must deal with the little foxes that are not readily visible. Do you have a little fox in your marriage or other relationships? Ask the Holy Spirit to help you destroy it before it destroys you and your home.

One of the fiery darts that Satan is quick to employ against marriages, especially when there is a heated conflict, is the satanic poison, the satanic arrow of accusation. Unfortunately, if care is not taken, our children suffer the collateral damage of spousal conflict. The satanic poison of accusation is given to our children to drink by their being exposed in the home to such unhealthy conflicts and sure enough, in the course of time, the eggs hatch and the children begin to manifest fear, guilt, insecurity, prejudice, and rejection. Satan is the accuser in the midst of the brethren, and he will use accusation as a bait. Christians who swallow the bait easily become a tool in the devil's hands.

Regarding marriages that have no more life in them, our Lord Jesus is still the Resurrection and the Life. He can make that dead marriage come alive again. For with God, nothing is impossible. Satan is the harbinger of death. He comes to steal, kill, and destroy *(John 10:10)* Christian marriages. Ephesians 4:27 admonishes us not to give the devil a foothold. This means we are not to create opportunities for him to work in our lives, including in our marriages. We must close all doors that have hitherto been opened to demonic forces so that they do not quickly convert footholds into strongholds. Until we keep Satan out of our marriages, our marriages will never know joy, peace, good health, and strength. Romans 14:17 states that the kingdom of God is not meat and drink, but righteousness, and peace, and joy in the Holy Ghost. Without righteousness in our marriages, we cannot have peace and joy. Matthew 6:33 tells us to seek first the kingdom of God and His righteousness and all "these" things shall be added unto us. These things include peace, joy, and healthy relationships.

The first step toward delivering a marriage from Satan's grip is for both spouses to walk in righteousness. If you are not walking in righteousness, you cannot have a righteous marriage with love, peace, joy, and understanding. Walking in righteousness requires genuine repentance, forgiveness, and humility. If we do not repent of sin, then sin will rule our marriages. If we do not forgive one another, then bitterness, anger, and resentment will remain in our hearts, and we will use these toxic things against our spouses and dump them in our marriages until they become an unmanageable pile. If we do not walk in humility, we will not see our need for deliverance and counseling. If we do not receive real deliverance, then demons that may be in us or around us have not been bound and cast out and may still have the opportunity to take the marriage on a downward slope again and again.

When a marriage has been under attack from satanic forces, there will often be a strong man assigned to quench the life out of that marriage. The strong man assigned to work against the marriage must be bound. It is this strong man that is responsible for making sure the husband and wife do not get along. The assignment of the strong man is to supervise division, strife, and hopelessness in a marriage. The strong man must be bound in the name of Jesus Christ and then in prayer you must begin to plunder his goods that he confiscated from you. Bind the strong man and take back your marriage from his control.

In working out the deliverance and healing of a troubled marriage, the husband and wife should submit themselves to deliverance and counseling. A competent deliverance pastor and marriage counselor should be sought. In addition, in the confines of their home, the couple can do deliverance on one another. The submitted wife can command demons in her husband to be bound and cast out in Jesus' name. The husband submitted to Christ should command demons in his wife to be bound and cast out in Jesus' name. Husband and wife should also do deliverance on the children so that if there be any demons in them, they too can be expelled. A demon-free home is a healthy home. Demons like to do their wicked work unnoticed. They do all they can to make their presence unknown. Demons work hard to see a husband and wife fighting and accusing one another while they escape being noticed for their input in the whole marital conflict. If demons are not detected, they escape the risk of being confronted and cast out in Jesus' name. Couples must learn to direct their fight not at themselves, but at the real enemy, Satan.

In some cultures, the man may be reluctant for his wife to do deliverance on him. The important thing to remember is that you are no longer under the rules and expectations of your culture—you are now in a new kingdom, the kingdom of God. In the kingdom of God, a man's wife is his helpmate. The helpmate can help cast out demons.

For deliverance of Christian marriages to be effective, an understanding of the root problems are paramount. Couples tend to mention the visible problems that are on the surface.

There are often root causes to those surface problems that are truly the real threats to a marriage. The roots give support and life to the surface problems. Once root problems are addressed and removed, the surface problems will begin to lose their chokehold. There is always a root cause to any marriage in crisis. The root may have grown even before the start of the marriage. Eventually, a tree producing the fruits of deceit and cheating may manifest in the marriage because the man or the woman carried those things before entering into marriage.

Deliverance of Christian marriages from the oppression of Satan will also require the family spending time together in prayer and Bible study. Christian couples should have daily devotions with prayer and meditation. With our busy schedules, it becomes increasingly challenging to fix a time as a family to always be with God in the home. The potency in this is that where two or more gather in the name of Christ, Christ is in their midst *(Matt. 18:20)*. As couples grow in the knowledge and in obedience to the Word of God, they are better equipped to keep out the devil from their marriages. God's Word is the Sword of the Spirit. This sword will chase out demonic forces. There is a saying that states, "The family that prays together, stays together." Consistent prayer and Bible study in a marriage help build a strong fence that the devil cannot penetrate in his attempt to plunder the marriage. A marriage with a strong hedge of protection will be immune from divorce. Building a strong hedge requires time and effort from both spouses. The weaker and unhealthier a marriage is, the more likely it could end in divorce if deliverance and counseling are not sought.

Christian marriages seem to be going in the direction of extinction. With the fierce manner in which forces of darkness have attacked them, more people have become reluctant to marry. They see marriage as a trap instead of a blessing. They see the casualties of failed marriages all around them and are fearful of being a statistic. In addition, the orientation of society has changed. Societal views of marriage have diminished the premium value placed on marriages before the sexual revolution of the 1960s.

There is the need for us to begin to take some practical biblical steps toward the healing of our marriages:

1. Forgiveness. This is essential for healing a marriage that has festering wounds. The parties must be willing to forgive regardless of who is at fault and the gravity of the offense.

2. Repentance. Unless there is genuine repentance, couples tend to keep indulging in the same destructive behaviors.

3. Humility. Apologize even if you are right for the sake of the peace.

4. Prayer. Husband and wife must consciously work on building a family altar where the entire family congregates to pray and study the Bible. We must constantly bind the strong man assigned against our marriages and ask the Lord to place a hedge of protection over them.

5. Self-control. As we work on restoring our marriages, we must die to self and live in the spirit. Spirit-filled people have self-control (this is a fruit of the Spirit) and can control their anger and speak with love and respect to their spouse even in the face of intense provocation.

As we invest in a lifestyle of godliness and introduce godly principles into our marriages, we keep our marriages out of the reach of Satan and his company of demons.

Prayers for Deliverance and Healing of Christian Marriages

Meditate on the following Scriptures: Ephesians 5:21–33; Mark 10:9; 1 Corinthians 7:10–11; and Proverbs 31:10–31, and pray these with all your heart:

1. In the name of Jesus, I bind the strong man assigned to destroy my marriage and destroy all his evil works by the power in the blood of Jesus.

2. In the name of Jesus, I command that any evil marriage in the spirit realm that is contending against my marriage on earth be destroyed by the fire of the Holy Spirit. In the name of Jesus, I disconnect myself and my spouse from any spiritual marriage to a spirit and ask for the fire of the Holy Spirit to destroy every object, vow, altar, demonic gift, and ceremony associated with such an evil marriage.

3. By the power in the blood of Jesus and in the name of Jesus, I destroy every witchcraft projection into my home and marriage designed to cause strife and confusion.

4. Let the angel of the Lord drive out every stranger assigned to frustrate my marriage in the name of Jesus.

5. I plead the blood of Jesus over my marriage.

6. Heavenly Father, release angels of peace, love, humility, and understanding into my home and marriage to heal, rebuild, and restore my marriage in Jesus' name.

7. Lord Jesus, I repent of every sin I have committed against my marriage vows and ask of your forgiveness.

8. Lord Jesus, let there be mutual forgiveness between my spouse and I as we receive your forgiveness.

9. Heavenly Father, put a hedge of protection around my marriage and keep demonic interference out in Jesus' name.

10. I reject every satanic alternative and counsel for my marriage in the name of Jesus.

8

FACILITATING DIVINE HEALING

[14]Is any sick among you? Let him call for the elders of the church; and let them pray over him, anointing him with oil in the name of the Lord: [15]And the prayer of faith shall save the sick, and the Lord shall raise him up; and if he have committed sins, they shall be forgiven him. [16]Confess your faults one to another, and pray one for another, that ye may be healed. The effectual fervent prayer of a righteous man availeth much *(James 5:14–16, KJV)*.

A question I have had to ask the Lord is this: Why is it that we have been praying for some for years, anointing the sick with oil in accordance with James 5:14, and have not seen the corresponding promise of healing assured in James 5:15–16? Many times we have fasted and prayed and held on to Scriptures on healing with great faith without experiencing healing. People are getting discouraged. Some are losing faith. A Christian friend once told me over the phone that he no longer believes that God is a healer because he has never seen any divine healing in his fifty years on earth. While not disputing what he had experienced in his lifetime, I vehemently disagreed with his conclusion. The Word of God cannot lie. God is not a man that he should lie; neither the son of man that he should repent: hath he said, and shall he not do it? Or hath he spoken, and shall he not make it good? *(Num. 23:19)*. I believe the Word of God wholeheartedly. Jesus Christ is the same yesterday, today, and forever *(Heb. 13:8)* and so is His word.

We are assured in 3 John 2 that God wills us to prosper and be in good health, even as our soul prospers. Jesus makes clear in the gospel that it is His will that the sick be healed. God's perfect will is that we be in good health and not experience any form of sickness or infirmity. Prevention, no doubt, is better than cure. Sickness does not bring glory to God. Healing and sound health bring glory to God. Sickness generally originates from the devil. The reason the Son of God was manifested was to destroy the works of the devil *(1 John 3:8)*. Nonetheless, God can send sickness as a result of disobedience. In Numbers 12 for instance, God inflicted Miriam with leprosy because of her rebellion against Moses.

Deuteronomy 28:58–61:

> [58] If you do not carefully follow all the words of this law, which are written in this book, and do not revere this glorious and awesome name—the Lord your God—
>
> [59] the Lord will send fearful plagues on you and your descendants, harsh and prolonged disasters, and severe and lingering illnesses.
>
> [60] He will bring on you all the diseases of Egypt that you dreaded, and they will cling to you.
>
> [61] The Lord will also bring on you every kind of sickness and disaster not recorded in this Book of the Law, until you are destroyed.

In Deuteronomy 28:58–61, God draws a connection between disobedience and disease. Most often, there is a connection between sin and sickness.

Praise the Lord, O my soul, and forget not all his benefits, who forgives all your sins and heals all your diseases *(Ps. 103:2–3)*.

In Psalm 103:3, the forgiveness of sins precedes the healing of diseases. In Mark 2, four men brought a paralytic lying on a mat to Jesus. Because of the crowds, the men had to make an opening in the roof and lower the mat the paralyzed man was on to get him to Jesus. When Jesus saw their faith, he said to the paralytic, "Son, your sins are forgiven" *(Mark 2:5)*. The first thing Jesus did was address the sins of the paralytic. The forgiveness of the paralytic's sins preceded his healing that was to follow. In the interim, between his sins being forgiven and the healing, people were saying in their hearts that Jesus was blaspheming because no one could forgive sins but God. Jesus demonstrated his authority to forgive sins by commanding the paralytic to be healed. In seeking deliverance from sickness and disease, we must address the issue of sin first. Sin and unforgiveness could be a major barrier that has stopped many from receiving their divine healing. In John 9, Jesus healed a man who was blind from birth. Jesus's disciples wanted to know the cause for the man being born blind. The disciples seemed to attribute his condition either to his sins or that of his parents. "Neither this man nor his parents sinned," said Jesus, "but this happened so that the work of God might be displayed in his life" *(John 9:3)*. In this case, there was no connection of sin to the disease in question.

Mark 5:25–34 narrates the story of the woman with the issue of blood for twelve years. Jesus was in the midst of the crowd and she pressed her way through and touched Jesus's garment because she believed that action would heal her. In response, Jesus said, "Daughter, your faith has healed you. Go in peace and be freed from your suffering" *(Mark 5:34)*. It is important to note that faith had been the means for the woman with the issue of blood to receive her healing, but Jesus was the source from which the healing was received.

In Exodus 15:26, God counsels the Israelites to abide in His Word to avoid diseases being placed upon them, and then He later reveals Himself as Jehovah Rapha—The Lord that healeth Thee. Jesus in the flesh was the physical embodiment of Jehovah Rapha. Jesus is the healer, and in the course of his earthly ministry, he never refused anyone that came to him to be healed. Those that were not healed by him are those that made no effort to come to him. The will of God regarding healing is expressed clearly in Luke 5:12–13:

> While Jesus was in one of the towns, a man came along who was covered with leprosy. When he saw Jesus, he fell with his face to the ground and begged him, "Lord, if you are willing, you can make me clean." Jesus reached out his hand and touched the man. "I am willing," he said. "Be clean!" And immediately the leprosy left him.

Later on, in Luke 9:1–2, we see Jesus authorizing and empowering his twelve disciples to subdue devils, cure diseases, preach, and heal the sick. This is the heart of God: that His people called by His name are healed and are in good health. Healing is the children's bread *(Matt. 15:26)*.

Mark 16:17–18:

> [17] And these signs will accompany those who believe: In my name they will drive out demons; they will speak in new tongues;
> [18] they will pick up snakes with their hands; and when they drink deadly poison, it will not hurt them

at all; they will place their hands on sick people, and they will get well."

Mark 16:18 lists one of the signs that follow believers as the laying of hands upon the sick for their recovery. Then why are we not witnessing much of these healings that Jesus talked about? This has led skeptics to doubt the fact that divine healing is taking place today. There is the need to properly and thoroughly document instances of divine healing so that no one gets the glory but the Healer, our Lord and Savior Jesus Christ.

Divine healing should be the norm and not the exception. Jesus Christ carried the sickness of mankind upon himself on the cross. By the stripes of Jesus Christ, we are healed *(Isa. 53:5)*. The Holy Spirit has given to some in the body of Christ, the gifts of healing *(1 Cor. 12:9)* for the benefit of the body of Christ *(1 Cor. 12:7)*. The school of thought that holds on to the position that divine healing and the gifts of healing are no longer in operation is in effect, denying the works and workings of the Holy Spirit today. The gifts of healing were given to build up the Church and glorify God. The Holy Spirit is still relevant today, and so the gifts and the fruits of the Holy Spirit are still working and evident in these end times.

> Verily, verily, I say unto you, He that believeth on me, the works that I do shall he do also; and greater works than these shall he do; because I go unto my Father *(John 14:12, KJV)*.

Jesus Christ provided the platform for man to be delivered from sickness and disease through the continuing work of the Holy Spirit. There are certain hindrances that stand in the way of our healing and that we will do well to remove, namely unforgiveness, failure to repent of sin, and lack of faith.

After we have ministered healing in the name of the Lord, some have come back to us with testimonies of healings to the astonishment of doctors. In our ministry, Overcomers in Christ Faith Assembly, we are still growing. There is so much to learn in this area, and we definitely cannot lay claim to a mastery of the knowledge in it. We are open to learning and growing, but there are some things the Lord has taught us and that is what I share here.

Ministering Divine Healing

In this area, the first thing we always look at is whether there are hindrances in the life of the person with the infirmity. We get the person to forgive all that have sinned against him and to ask for God's forgiveness. We share Scriptures on healing with the person to build up their faith for their healing. Romans 10:17 says, "So then faith cometh by hearing, and hearing by the word of God."

Many infirmities and ailments are caused by demons, and discernment will be needed to know if a demon is at work. In Luke 13 we see that the physical condition of a woman was caused by a spirit of infirmity, which is released after Jesus lays his hands on her:

> And behold, there was a woman which had a spirit of infirmity eighteen years, and was bowed together, and could in no wise lift up herself. And when Jesus saw her, he called her to him, and said unto her, Woman, thou art loosed from thine infirmity. And he laid his hands on her: and immediately she was made straight, and glorified God *(Luke 13: 11–13, KJV).*

In Mark 9:17–29, Jesus casts out a dumb and deaf spirit from a boy that had previously thrown him to the ground, made him foam at the mouth, gnash his teeth, and become rigid. As soon as the spirit is cast out, the boy is made whole. Jesus accomplished many healings by casting out demons.

In ministering divine healing, we must probe to see if there is any demonic connection to the condition. Once there is a spiritual root or connection behind the disease, we must bind and cast out the strong man of infirmity with the assignment of enforcing that infirmity in the life of the afflicted. In accomplishing this, we must break generational covenants and curses to destroy whatever legal rights or legal hold the demons may have in asserting the infirmity. All spirits associated with these curses and covenants of infirmity must be bound and cast out as well. The evil spirits must be firmly commanded to leave the afflicted person in the name of Jesus.

After clearing these prerequisites, the next thing to do is to minister divine healing according to James 5:13–16. This requires that we lay hands on the sick person in the name of Jesus, anointing the person with oil and then bind the strong man and associated demons in the name of Jesus and by the power of the Holy Spirit. After this, with authority we command the demon perpetuating the sickness to release the afflicted person in the name of Jesus. Infirmity is like a mountain, and Mark 11:23 instructs us to say to the mountain "Go throw yourself into the sea" without doubting what we have said, it shall be so. Saying and praying are two different things. There is a time to pray and a time to talk to the mountain. At the mention of the name of Jesus, sickness and infirmity must bow. At the close of prayers, it is good to thank the Lord for the healing that has been prayed for and received in faith. When all these are done in righteousness and faith, healing is eminent and will eventually manifest. The enemy may counterattack with lies to the effect that the healing is a sham. The devil will release lying spirits to create doubt in the mind of the afflicted that no real healing took place. The afflicted must stand his ground in Christ and resist and rebuke every lying spirit sent to steal his healing. Yes, God is sovereign, and He can decide when and if a healing will take place. Nonetheless, this we have found to be a Bible-based approach to minister and receive healing.

Prayers for Divine Healing

Meditate on the following Scriptures: Exodus 15:26; Psalm 41:4; Isaiah 53:5; Luke 4:18; Acts 10:38; and James 5:13–18. Pray the following:

1. In the name of Jesus and by the power of the Holy Spirit, I bind the strong man of infirmity assigned to attack me and establish infirmity in my life.
2. In the name of Jesus, I plead the blood of Jesus against every root of infirmity that has inhabited my body and command it to loose me now.
3. In the name of Jesus, I repent of every sin that has given spirits of infirmity access into my life and take back all grounds yielded to powers of darkness.
4. In the name of Jesus, I break and loose myself from all demonic subjection to sicknesses inherited from my ancestors.
5. I reject every sickness upon me imposed by witchcraft powers upon me and command every arrow of affliction to return to their evil senders in Jesus' name.
6. I break every curse and covenant of infirmity working against me and my household and bind all spirits associated with these curses and covenants in Jesus' name.
7. I command with authority every demon perpetuating sickness in my body to be cast out now in the name of Jesus.
8. I command every spirit manifesting as (name symptom, e.g., diabetes, cancer, arthritis, etc.) in my body to come out of me now in Jesus' name. Let the

blood of Jesus wash away every symptom in Jesus' name.

9. I command any sickness in me that has confounded the doctors and that has evaded diagnosis and detection to be consumed by fire in the name of Jesus.

10. Heavenly Father, send forth Your Word to heal my disease and save me from destruction in the name of Jesus.

9

DELIVERANCE FROM HOUSE OF SATAN (A PERSONAL TESTIMONY)

The steps of a good man are ordered by the Lord: and he delighteth in his way *(Ps. 37:23, KJV)*.

Oftentimes, it is in retrospect that one is able to appreciate the reasons for one's life trials and experiences. It is when one takes a look back that he begins to see God's record of faithfulness. God takes us through different courses and channels to prepare us for the work and the things He has had in mind for us to do before the foundation of the world. While we may be busy going about our own business of ignoring the Lord or rebelling against Him, the Lord is busy working to bring us to the place of our divine calling and assignment. When the Lord calls, He is looking for those that will respond, "Here am I." As I have worked in the pastoral ministry and as a deliverance minister, I have often looked back over my life and seen better and more clearly now how indeed all things work together for the good of those that love God and are called according to His purpose *(Rom. 8:28)*. Those that love God can only love God for the simple reason that He first loved them *(1 John 4:19)*. God's love is demonstrated toward us in that while we were yet sinners, Christ died for us *(Rom. 5:8)*. Christ went to the cross and paid the ultimate price for us even when we were against Him. That is great love and greater love has no man than this, that a man lay down his life for his friends *(John 15:13)*. Whatever we are and whatever we become is simply by His grace.

> For we are God's workmanship, created in Christ Jesus to do good works, which God prepared in advance for us to do *(Eph. 2:10)*.

The good works we do now for Christ were prepared in advance by God. God also prepares us for the work He has in mind. He will allow us to go through hills and valleys, crises and comfort so that when it is time for our work, we will be ready. For God to use Moses to bring out His people, the Israelites, from bondage, He had to take Moses from Pharaoh's palace, where he had completed the lessons for that phase of his life, into the deserts to be a shepherd. Shepherds lead sheep, and people are like sheep. Moses had to go through that obscure phase of being a shepherd in order to qualify as God's leader for God's people. In making a pastor and deliverance worker, God trained me from my youth without my even realizing it.

In my high-school years at King's College Lagos, I debated for the school. Interschool debate competitions require a lot of preparation and confidence to speak before an audience. These are qualities that will also help a pastor succeed in ministry. I had studied law in the University of Benin, Nigeria, and later completed a master's degree in commercial and corporate law at King's College London in 1990. The study of law at the university level gives one a very analytical and inquisitorial mind, which also is a quality that could help a pastor succeed in ministry, especially in exposition and in counseling.

In my twenties, I lived, studied, and worked on four continents, namely, Africa, Europe, Asia, and North America. I also visited a number of countries. Again, I look back in retrospect, and I see that this experience of mixing with multiple cultures has given me some leverage to minister across cultural lines. In the late 1980s and early 1990s, my father was Nigeria's ambassador to South Korea, and once in a while he would insist I accompany him for some diplomatic dinner or cocktail or other function of the sort. As a young man, I dreaded attending these parties because I felt out of place. The more the diplomats from other foreign countries tried to make me feel comfortable, the more out of place I felt. To me, I was in an artificial environment. I vowed never to be an ambassador like my dad. Today, I am an ambassador for Jesus Christ representing Christ wherever I go. Even though the world is hostile to Christ, I still must represent Him. It is amazing how God uses these kinds of experiences to prepare us for tasks ahead. It is little wonder that the relatively small church I pastor in Brooklyn, New York, consists of believers from at least fifteen nations, spanning Europe, Asia, Africa, the West Indies, South America, and North America.

In my twenties, from 1991 through 1993, I also taught law briefly in two major universities in Nigeria; and my experience as a law teacher has helped me in the pastoral ministry. Pastors are teachers of the Word of God. I do recognize that it is not my abilities that qualify me for ministry, but nonetheless these experiences have helped me relate to people from different walks of life. While the above-mentioned experiences may be viewed as somewhat elitist, they have prepared me to minister to the elites alike, including those who would find it more difficult to enter heaven than a camel would through the eye of a needle. Yet there are some dreadful experiences the Lord has allowed me to go through that have helped me relate to all regardless of class or social status. In the eyes of God, the things man sees as important are vanity. We must all learn to look at people through His eyes.

By 1990, I had drifted back and forth from atheism to agnosticism. I grew up in the Anglican Church (Episcopalian) but had never had a relationship with Jesus Christ. I did not care whether God even existed. In January 1992, I was introduced and initiated into a marine occult house in Lagos called the Sea Lodge. My going there in the first place was as a result of my curiosity and my inflated ego that wanted to assure itself that there was nothing like supernatural phenomena, and thus there were no divine actors like God or the devil. Before I could probe any further, I was made to enter into an oath with life-and-death consequences should I violate the oath. The oath was that if I were to reveal matters of the Sea Lodge or leave the Sea Lodge, I would die in a car accident or be paralyzed for life. I threw caution to the wind and took the oath. After taking it in one of the Sea Lodge shrines in the Alapere-Ketu area of Lagos, to my astonishment questionable powers began to arrive at the shrine. These powers were the seven spirits of the Sea Lodge, wicked demons that resided in the belly of the sea. The Sea Lodge also invoked spirits from India and a very powerful demon called the Queen of the Coast. The latter was requested when there were serious matters at stake.

So amidst fear and fright, I was drafted into this body along with three other new recruits. At initiation, I met Dr. Eli from the riverine area of eastern Nigeria. He was a top spiritist of the Sea Lodge. He communed with spirits from India, the seven spirits of the Sea Lodge, and once in a while, the Queen of the Coast. I was amazed at how these invisible spirit entities knew my life history in the minutest of details. They were right on target about virtually all of my past and present. They seemed to have a knowledgeable insight of what the future might hold for me. All my life, and prior to this experience, I had processed and evaluated information through empirical and objective means. Now I was confounded by powers that did not go through the same process but seemed to know much more than the rest of mankind. I thought, *Perhaps these fairytales we read as children have some reality behind them after all.* These demons from the sea promised me wealth and fame so long as I danced to their bidding. In the course of time, the conditions they put on their favors were beyond my ethical capacity, and I had to back down from pursuing this course that only leads to eternal death and damnation.

In the course of my journey, I recall visiting a man gifted in things of the spirit in my hometown of Benin City. This man went by the name of "Uncle B." I needed some form of independent confirmation of what I was being told in Lagos by the Sea Lodge. To my amazement, he repeated the exact same things concerning my future that I had heard in Lagos. This independent insight from Uncle B served as some sort of verification and made me realize solemnly for the first time that the spirit world is real. Any assumptions I had of a fantasy spirit world were now out the door! Much of the operations and activities of the Sea Lodge were shrouded in secrecy. One member may not be privy to what another member is doing, but the spirits monitored all Sea Lodge activities entrusted to men. I knew that the Sea Lodge was evil. Its deeds and pronouncement of judgments had no iota of mercy in them. It now became obvious to me that if there is this domain of darkness and evil, then there must be a domain of light and good. In my case, because I had a stubborn and unyielding heart, God had to show me the enemy and what he stood for before He could reveal Himself to me.

The spiritist mediums of the Sea Lodge never did seem comfortable with the name "Jesus." They always approached that name with fear and trepidation or with outright expression of annoyance. Many in the Sea Lodge insisted that church was a farce considering that a number of church leaders in Nigeria came and pled with the sea for power and prosperity. If others had to plead and beg for prosperity from these custodians of evil, I then began to wonder why I was being offered such treasures on a platter of gold. After ensuring that I was fairly entrenched in the Sea Lodge, I was then made to learn of the conditions precedent for receiving my so-called gift. Indeed, the thief cometh not but to steal, kill, and destroy.

At times, the demon designated as the spirit mother would speak clearly and at other times, faintly. The demons announced that I was the leader of a new group of initiated converts. As a new group, we met in a swampy forest situated in the outskirts of Lagos. The so-called spirit mother called my name, "Idemudia," in such a sweet, loving, melodious, and affectionate tone I had never heard before. It was so captivating, so enchanting. This encounter gave me a false sense of security that these demonic beings actually loved and cared for me. As a group of new converts, we had to each take the individual oath of secrecy, which I mentioned before, that if we ever revealed the source of our prospective wealth, we would be killed in a car accident or be paralyzed for life. As a leader, the seven spirits of the Sea Lodge directed that I use part of the prospective wealth, which was approximately eighty thousand US dollars at the time, to build a community center in Benin City. When I heard this idea of a community center, I was deluded into thinking these demons cared for mankind and wanted to see an improvement in the lot of our people.

As I was getting more engrossed in the Sea Lodge, I had a very clear and unambiguous dream. I was sleeping in my room in my parents' home in Benin City. In that dream, a man called me into a big hall. His face and eyes were shining. He told me, as if commanding me, to go and sin no more. I just knew that this was Jesus. He needed no introduction. He exhibited so much peace, compassion, and authority. He impressed me as someone who was on a mission. He did not give me the time or opportunity to confront or negotiate with him. It was not that I could have said anything to Him anyway because I was so awed and dwarfed by His presence. When I woke up, I pondered this. I chose to ignore

Jesus. After all, I too had an agenda to accomplish. I could not mention this dream to the Sea Lodge because it would have made them angry and suspicious of me. When Jesus appeared to me in my dream, the demons from the sea were nowhere to be found. Sometimes, the Sea Lodge would ask if I had any dream, and I would just tell them "no." By God's grace I got away with this lie to powers that seemed to know everything and punish everything.

In late 1992 or early 1993, I met an interesting stranger on a commercial bus in Benin City that I had randomly chosen to enter. He introduced himself as Alhaji and informed me that my wealth had arrived from underneath the sea. To play safe and protect my position, I insisted that I did not know what he was talking about. First, I did not know who he was and second, of course, I had taken an oath with severe penalties not to reveal Sea Lodge matters to strangers. I later came to understand that Alhaji had mystic powers given to him by the kingdom of darkness. Satan has an army of human agents eager to do his bidding. He has given many mystical powers in exchange for their souls.

The generality of mankind has labored under the illusion that Satan is a very ugly being. Actually, this is a false belief created by darkness. The Bible, in Ezekiel 28:12, describes Satan as being created as a model of perfection, full of wisdom and perfect in beauty. Further along, in verse 17, we see that Satan's heart became proud on account of his beauty and that he corrupted his wisdom because of his splendor. Satan has promised many of his human followers not only power and riches on earth, but rewards after death. These followers have eaten deep from the tree of the knowledge of good and evil, and so they are enthralled by the beauty, power, and promises of Satan. Unfortunately, what these people do not understand is that Satan is a die-hard deceiver, defeated by the One known as Jesus Christ.

Satan's eternity is in the lake of fire. He cannot deliver on his promises. Even if he had the willingness to fulfill promises of rewards after death, he lacks the capacity to do so. In Revelation 20, we see this Satan being confined to a bottomless pit for a thousand years and then thrown into a lake of burning sulfur for all of eternity. What promise, reward, or benefit does anyone expect to receive from Satan? These human agents such as witches, warlocks, sorcerers, alchemists, spiritists, psychics, Satanists, and false prophets are as deceived as the grand deceiver that they worship.

As a principal beneficiary of the riches, I chose a collection date. On the day of collection, we couldn't receive even though the container of wealth and the demonic spirits of the Sea Lodge were present. It appears that God used the June 12, 1993, election political crisis and attendant riots in Lagos and other parts of Nigeria to frustrate our purpose. Despite the fact that traveling from Benin to Lagos, a distance of about two hundred miles, was very unsafe and the means of transportation in the country was severely limited by the political upheavals of the time, the Sea Lodge still expected us to report as scheduled. To them, an agreement was an agreement irrespective of the circumstances.

I showed up a bit late, but a colleague could not make it, owing to the riots and confusion in Lagos. The spirits had no sympathy and fined us a carton of Seaman's Aromatic Schnapps for my failure to keep the appointment on time and for my colleague's nonappearance. The spirits were bent on punishing and tormenting us for any slight infraction or mistake, forgetting that we were only human. Inwardly, I began to question my allegiance to this organization. As I noted before, withdrawing from the Sea Lodge carried the death penalty or paralysis for life. I was now in the heart of the lion's den. The lions were roaring and becoming even more frightening. In the course of history, very few mortals have survived the onslaught of a pack of lions. Those that survived really had a story to tell. With the exception of Daniel, kept from harm by the only true and living God, no other came out unscathed. Like every soldier in fierce combat, I have a number of bruises from my encountering and dining with invisible powers beyond my comprehension. I had to come out with a plan of escape. The plan was deeply embedded in the cross of Christ. The only way I knew of escape was to turn to the One who appeared to me so clearly and distinctly in my dream, the Lord and Savior Jesus Christ. This was still to be awhile though.

After bargaining and a lull, I made it clear to the Sea Lodge that I could not work with them if they failed to demonstrate faithfulness in honoring their own promises. Their lies and refusal to keep their promises resulted in a deadlock. It was now becoming clearer to me that the Sea Lodge wanted other things to keep me permanently ensnared. They wanted my soul or that of a close relative, preferably an innocent child, in exchange for the riches already credited to my account in the domain of darkness. They intended to break us down to the last crumb so that we would voluntarily offer our souls to redeem our station in life. This breaking down and the accompanying rise in fortune served as a reminder to human beneficiaries of the Sea Lodge that whatever they were in life, they owed it to the seven spirits of the Sea Lodge.

A flood of fear and despair now overwhelmed me. In my limited human perception at the time, I had seen the spirits perform magic and inconceivable wonders in my very sober and conscious presence. I knew there was no way I could fight them alone. In the course of these particularly trying times, I had stopped entertaining the idea that I engineered my own destiny. Now, for the first time in my life, I had reached a point where I truly did not know what else to do. I was absolutely unwilling to give a human sacrifice or exchange my soul for anything. The Sea Lodge tripled the amount of riches. I knew I could not go on any longer with them. In 1991, when

I had returned to Nigeria from the Far East, my vision was to undertake research work in Nigerian universities and then apply to do a PhD in an area of commercial law in either the United Kingdom or United States. I put this vision on hold to pursue a seemingly promising future backed by nothing other than demons. The realization that neither objective would be attainable only helped fuel my sense of hopelessness and frustration. My indulgence in alcohol and tobacco had also grown in alarming proportions. And of course, with all these came a loss of values and concern.

One evening in Benin City, my father summoned me into his living room. He expressed concern with how I was losing the fine qualities I had always been known to embrace. I am my father's last son, and he had always demonstrated so much unselfish love toward me. I recalled him saying something to the effect that I, his magnificent pearl, was now becoming like sour grapes before him. Dad is one gentleman that rarely talks, but when he does talk, it has to be taken seriously. He had excelled in learning with a PhD in physics from the University of Pittsburgh in 1966. He had excelled in the Nigerian civil service, administration, and in politics, rising to the position of ambassador extraordinary and plenipotentiary of the Federal Republic of Nigeria. My dad is that kind of man who does much more listening than talking, but when he talked, he got so much attention. Now, he had called me in for a talk, and I felt like a dwarf before him. He advised me with words of wisdom and old age. Rather than listen to him, I kept arguing with him and accusing him of unnecessary interference. Like Pontius Pilate, he then sought to wash his hands clean concerning me. However, my mother would not accept his thought of giving up on me. She became very emotional and prevailed on my father to give me more chances and to work with me. I just couldn't wait for this meeting with my parents to be over so that I could go seek relief in my beer and cigarettes, which were now my constant daily companions.

In mid-1993, Nigeria was virtually shut down. My place of employment, the university, was closed down by the military authorities. By September 1993, I left Nigeria for the United States. During this lull, I kept recalling the encounter I had with Jesus Christ in my dream of late 1992 in my bedroom in Benin City. I wondered how come the Sea Lodge did not pick up on this dream. After all, they boasted that they had access to every power in the universe because the seas and waters were so strategic. During this time, I began to read the Bible to better understand who Jesus is. The Bible gave me a renewed kind of hope I could not yet define. I drank and I smoked and I still read my Bible regularly and more frequently. I enjoyed reading the gospels and the psalms. In them, I found a degree of peace. In them, my faith in God began to emerge. It was only a matter of time for me to make that commitment of surrender to Jesus Christ.

In January 1994 or thereabout, I replied to a letter from the Sea Lodge informing them of my decision to quit the lodge and forfeit the combination of riches. Once again, the implication of this, according to these lying spirits, was death in an automobile accident or paralysis for life. I severed all forms of communication with the Sea Lodge, its demons and agents. I would not be surprised if this community of demons still harbors plans to execute my demise and see me live in misery. The seven spirits of the Sea Lodge had made it clear that if their treacherous gift was refused, my colleagues and I would be wretched in life without money or property. A curse would be pronounced on us were we to reject the "gift."

Well, I rejected their gift in absolute terms. I rejected their gift that leads to everlasting damnation in hellfire. This was no gift. This was a burden. In placing my faith in Christ, I accepted the free gift of salvation that leads to everlasting life. The blood of Christ prevails over every work of darkness exemplified by the Sea Lodge, an instrument and tool of iniquity in the hands of the devil. What a relief it is to be no longer bound and subject to these evil powers. Indeed, it is such a joyous blessing to be free.

> Praise be to the Lord, who has not let me be torn by their teeth. I have escaped like a bird out of the fowler's snare; the snare has been broken and I have escaped (*Ps. 124: 6–7*).

I had been to the lions' den and come out alive. I believe God's Word that no weapon fashioned against me shall prosper. Romans 8:31 assures me that if God be for me, no one can stand against me. If the Sea Lodge wants to reach me or deal with me, it will have to go through my lawyer and advocate, Jesus Christ. For those that believe, Jesus Christ is our high priest that sits at the right hand of God the Father, forever making intercession for us. Hebrews chapters 4, 5, and 7, among others, highlight the priestly ministry of Jesus Christ. What a friend we have in Jesus. The Sea Lodge would have to pass the cross of Calvary, where I was redeemed, in order to reach me. And I know that that is a ground they dare not tread upon. With the help of God, I had fought and won this battle described in Ephesians 6:12. Yes, my heel was bruised, but the head of the enemy was crushed. There were still more battles waiting to be fought. I have never stopped fighting because I have never stopped believing. The kingdom of darkness is always determined to strike back in the course of a struggle; but we that are in Christ Jesus are more than overcomers and conquerors.

> Who will rise up for me against the wicked? Who will take a stand for me against evildoers? Unless the Lord had given me help, I would have soon dwelt in the silence of death. When I said "my foot is slipping," your love, O Lord supported me. When anxiety was

great within me, your consolation brought joy to my soul *(Ps. 94:16–18)*.

Psalm 137:1–4, KJV:

¹ By the rivers of Babylon, there we sat down, yea, we wept, when we remembered Zion.
² We hanged our harps upon the willows in the midst thereof.
³ For there they that carried us away captive required of us a song; and they that wasted us required of us mirth, saying, Sing us one of the songs of Zion.
⁴ How shall we sing the Lord's song in a strange land?

Life is intriguing. We struggle to build and achieve success only to see others determined to destroy what we have built, like the World Trade Center towers that were toppled in 2001. The year 2005 ushered me into my own Ground Zero. It was in this year that my life was stretched to the breaking point. I was broken, but I did not break into pieces. God held me. Here is my story:

By the end of 2004, I had attained significant success for my age of thirty-seven years. I had my own home, my own family, a few investments, and was developing my own business. In early 2005, I fled from an irredeemable marriage: with hindsight and spiritual oversight, I came to understand that from the very beginning, this marriage was destined for failure. As an alien in the United States who had suffered untold miscarriages of justice at the hands of the United States Citizenship and Immigration Services, I couldn't depend on any American system to give me justice. Justice in America, to an extent, is political and biased. The family legal system seems biased in favor of the women, more so when the man is an alien whose legal status in the US is being challenged.

It would have been naïve of me to think that I could get a fair hearing or substantive justice by having recourse to my accusers, the immigration authorities who had done me so much irreversible harm as a result of their own recklessness.

Leaving this marriage meant that I stood the risk of losing my son and real and personal properties I had worked for. I was determined to minimize my risks and maximize whatever minute advantages I had. My exit from the matrimonial home was painstakingly executed and unfortunately brought hardship and inconveniences to my wife and son. For the hardship and inconvenience, I am truly sorry. Nonetheless, it was a task that had to be done, as I felt I was being choked and constricted within the confines of my marriage.

Upon my departure from my matrimonial home, my wife, an American citizen, knowing full well the ordeal I had endured with the US Citizenship and Immigration Services, wrote to them to cancel my application for permanent residency in the United States. She had sponsored a petition on my behalf for my immigration status to be changed to "permanent resident." Her canceling the petition and accusing me of all forms of wrongdoing further compounded my immigrant status dilemma. At this point, and not surprisingly, all my alien privileges were either revoked or denied by US Citizenship and Immigration Services. That meant that I no longer had the right to work and earn a living in the US. It meant that if I left the US for any reason, I could not return to even see my son.

In the midst of all this personal turmoil, I began to fight more aggressively in the spirit. In August 2005, I fasted and prayed for one week. The spiritual battles became more intense as I began to take authority over demons.

Without any means of supply and support, by October 2005 I was practically destitute. I had suffered severe financial loss, loss of profitable employment, and a partial heart failure. I was admitted to the hospital for my heart disease and without any form of health insurance and with a shaky immigration status, I had to bear the astronomical costs of this hospitalization. By the time I was discharged, I was weak and fragile and continued to suffer more losses. For about seven months, I had no telephone and depended on public payphones to make important calls. I lost communication with so many people and was separated from many in the course of my trials. This separation drew me nearer to the presence of God. Usually when God wants a man's undivided attention, He separates him from distractions from all sides.

As the winter of 2005/2006 approached, I was not prepared for it. Without sufficient heat in the room I had rented, it was the grace of God that kept me from another return to the hospital. The hardships of 2005 certainly drew me closer to my God, my Lord and Savior Jesus Christ. In the midst of sufferings and deprivation, I had such a wonderful time with Jesus Christ. Christ sent His ministers into my life to encourage and strengthen me in the faith.

My faith in God transcended every conceivable hardship. Intense trials are nothing more than tests designed to show us where we are and to make us stronger. The biblical book of James 1 is very instructive on human trials. In James 1:2–4, we are encouraged to consider it pure joy whenever we face trials of many kinds because the testing of our faith develops perseverance. Perseverance must finish its work so that we become mature and complete, not lacking anything. In verse 12, we see that blessed is the man who perseveres under trial, because when he has stood the test, he will receive the crown of life that God has promised to those who love Him.

Trials are opportunities for us to be elevated to a higher level of achievement. It takes enduring faith coupled with the grace of God to go through a gruesome trial and maintain composure of peace and joy. My faith in God assures me that everything will be alright. It assures me that all things work together for the good of those that love God and are called according to His purpose. In every trial and in everyday life, I walk by faith and not by what I see or hear. If you are moved by what you see and what you hear, then you are one who is easily moved. All the enemy need do is put something before you to impress you to move. Oftentimes, fear of the unknown makes man make decisions that are not for his own benefit. This is a form of engaging in "short term gain for long term pain." As a series of trials approached, faith in God was ready to chase the forces of darkness out. In Ephesians 6:16, we see that faith is a shield that quenches the sting, the venom, and the fire in the enemy's arsenal. In other words, faith neutralizes the enemy's advances against God's people. In 1 John 5:4, it is made clear that the victory that overcomes the world is embedded in our faith.

The hallmark definition of faith is contained in Hebrews 11:1. It says that faith is the substance of things hoped for and the evidence of things not seen. To assess one's faith, a few questions may prove critical. These are questions such as the following: What am I hoping for? Am I really hoping for it to be substantiated? What is it that I do not see and yet expect to see materialize? Do I really expect to see it materialize? The evidence of things not seen is faith. The evidence of things not seen, but hoped for, is revealed by how we live our lives, especially in times of severe trials. As Proverbs 24:10 puts it, "If you falter in times of trouble, how small is your strength!" If you faint in the day of adversity, your strength is small. In other words, if you are slack in your day of distress, it shows the weakness of your supposed strength. It takes faith in God and the grace of God to withstand the pressures of adversity. In these last days we need the faith that can believe God for anything, including the impossible. It is in the intense heat and fires of adversities that one's faith is stretched to new limits.

As I lay on my bed very early in the morning of February 2, 2006, two demons entered my room. I was fully awake.

The first one took the form of a beautiful young lady and lay next to me on my bed. The second demon lay on the floor by the other side of my bed. The demon on the bed said, "We'll just hang out here for a while." Immediately, in my spirit, I detected foul play. My mouth was sealed, and I could not talk or fight out in speech. I started praying in the spirit, rebuking them in the name of Jesus, and directing the thunder fire of the Holy Ghost against them. As this was going on, I regained the ability to open my mouth, and I continued calling on Jesus Christ. The demons disappeared. Once again, Christ had defeated powers of darkness.

This was no surprise as I was no longer a stranger to such encounters. I recall prior to this incident having a somewhat similar spiritual experience on May 19, 2005. Around 8:30 a.m., I lay in bed awake. An audible voice spoke directly to my ear saying that I should pay off the devil with money so that he would leave me alone. I tried to speak up and say no, but could not. It was as if my mouth and body were tied. Eventually, the voice left and I pled the blood of Jesus.

Two significant events occurred in my life in April 2006. That month, I became completely homeless. In that same month, I was also ordained a pastor of the Gospel Missionary Church (GMC) in Brooklyn, New York. As associate pastor, I was responsible for the Wednesday Bible study and the Friday night prayer meetings.

The Spirit of God, in the midst of my trials, backed me up so strongly with such remarkable anointing. In a few months, attendance at church weekly activities approached Sunday church-service attendance. People were hungry for the power of God. We had seen God respond to our prayers and knew that God was in control.

From April through June 2006, I made the floors of the church sanctuary my bed. I had to go to several places in New York to have a bath. I spent three months in the church with only a very few people knowing of my homeless condition.

With the help of God, the peace, the joy, and the faith of God in me kept increasing. From my prayer band days at the Brooklyn Tabernacle in 1997, I had grown into a radical prayer warrior. Whoever thought that my becoming homeless would mark my downfall was wrong. God just changed my address to His church. When a committed prayer warrior is stuck in the House of God for three consecutive months, things begin to happen. Eventually, I was able to get a job as a parking attendant in a Manhattan garage, barely earning the minimum wage. I thanked God for my job. Now, with a little income in hand, I was determined to get out of my homeless situation as quickly as possible.

I had fallen down to Ground Zero. At Zero, I always was encouraged by the meaning of my first name, "Idemudia." Idemudia is a Nigerian name of Benin origin meaning "triumphant in adversity." Literally, it means the one that gets up at a fall. It connotes victory and implies strength. With divine help, I was fully persuaded that I would triumph over every adversity. I often found encouragement in Psalm 34:19, which states that many are the afflictions of the righteous, but the Lord delivers him out of them all.

By July 2006, I found a room to rent in a three-bedroom apartment in the rougher parts of the South Bronx. As I moved into my new abode, which I shared with two other occupants—I had my own room, and they occupied the others—I began to wonder whether I had done the right thing. I had lived in New York for ten years and nothing had prepared me for this new neighborhood. It was a tremendous culture shock. The noise level was so provocative even at midnight, three a.m., or whatever time of the day. Crime was rampant. Drug abuse, teenage pregnancies, and gang-related fights dominated my new environment. I felt so unsafe. My roommates were so inconsiderate and held parties during the day and at night. They would use up my food and drinks and not replace them. I held my peace.

In my new home, my routine was such that I worked the night shift in the garage and needed to catch a few hours of sleep during the day. Once in a while, I got home early in the morning by nine, only to meet a party going on or just winding down. The music would be so loud that I entertained no thought of sleeping. If the music was not loud, they were screaming and shouting at the top of their lungs. At times, I would enter the shared apartment and meet a good number of people smoking hemp. The police had been to the apartment once or twice, and I was fortunate to have been at work in the garage at the times of their visits. Fortunately, after a few months, I was able to get another one-room apartment in the same building. I moved out as quickly as I could to this new room. It was quiet and relatively peaceful. Here, I had much more reasonable and responsible roommates.

But I must tell you about the night I moved out from my old room. It was very interesting. I moved out as these lousy roommates of mine were having a noisy party. The apartment was filled with strangers; a few were smoking pot openly and alcohol was freely flowing. I was thankful to God that I was escaping this arena of insanity in one piece. I was determined to move to a quieter neighborhood as soon as I had the means.

I kept crying out to God for a breakthrough in these times of severe testing. My weekly income from the garage was a paltry sum of two hundred eighty dollars. My weekly rent was one hundred fifteen dollars. My transportation costs on a weekly basis were twenty-four dollars. I paid a weekly tithe of thirty dollars. By the time I deducted feeding and other daily expenses, I was back at zero dollars at the end of the week. God had to intervene, and I knew He would. My question was not whether God would intervene on my behalf. My question was when.

I kept asking myself what an attorney was doing parking cars in a garage for slightly more than the minimum wage. Everything in life has a purpose and a reason. What was God's purpose in all these? I felt like Job, who went from something to nothing overnight. A man who once had a five-bedroom house of his own had now tasted homelessness and been reduced to renting a fourteen-foot by twelve-foot room. A man who once owned cars could not afford to own a bicycle. Yet God was telling me that all was well. I believed God in spite of the gloom that surrounded me. There are things you learn in a garage that you could never learn in a law office. I learned about people based on the cars they drove and how they kept them. Peter, an Italian-American gentleman in his early sixties, parked his car in the garage. It was well kept, almost spotless. I saw Christian literature in his car and began to suspect that he might be a Christian. I saw his humble demeanor and waited for a Saturday morning when the garage was quiet to discuss my faith with him. Peter was a Christian! His influence in my life was such a blessing. He took the time to pray with me and encourage me. Sometimes he brought food, sometimes he brought clothing, and other times he gave money. Peter had demonstrated true Christian living, and I knew he was someone I could confide in.

One of the most well-known passages in the Bible is found in Psalm 23. Only after David passes through the valley of the shadow of death in verse 4 is a table prepared for him in the midst of his enemies in verse 5. God is good at beautifying lives in the valley. He gets our attention when we are stationed in the low and lonely places of life. God leads us to the valley. He may or may not use our enemies to push us to the valley. One thing is certain though, and that is that God will humiliate the enemies of His people by showing His approval and benevolence. He will prepare a table for us in the presence of our enemies. I consider it a privilege to have been visited by extreme trials. They have only made me stronger and drawn me closer to God. From Genesis to Revelation in the Bible, we see that every great man of God was baptized in the crucibles of trials. It is in these trials that God's power is revealed more clearly. Every time I read Hosea 2:14–16, I see more clearly how God chooses to work in the lives of His people. God in speaking to His people through the Prophet Hosea declared thus:

> [14] Therefore, I am now going to allure her; I will lead her into the desert and speak tenderly to her.
> [15] There I will give her back her vineyards, and will make the valley of Achor a door of hope. There she will sing as in the days of her youth, as in the day she came up out of Egypt.
> [16] "In that day," declares the Lord, "you will call me 'my husband'; you will no longer call me 'my master.' "

In verse 14 above, we see that it is God who orchestrated His people's entry into the desert. You see, the desert is a place of extreme scarcity, deprivation, and isolation. God leads His people into this place so He can get their full attention. In the desert, God speaks tenderly to them. In verse 15, we see a restoration taking place. When one has passed through the desert, he is able to handle the proceeds of restoration wisely and prudently. When one goes through the desert, he needs no one to teach him not to waste water anymore. As God continues working in the lives of His people, they have new hope and begin rejoicing with singing. A man who does not lose his song in the deepest of trials is a man who has not lost his faith. In verse 16, we see a new relationship being forged between God and the people that have been processed in the desert.

One interesting thing about being in the desert is that you really begin to know who is truly on your side and who is not. The people who are genuinely called to be with you will always be available when you need them. Those that God is trying to weed out of your life will now be nowhere to be found. The desert is a weeding out process. It was in the desert that I saw what a true friend Joseph Boateng was indeed. Joseph stood by me through thick and thin. He was a man earning a meager income and yet he chose to support me consistently. He supported me when I was an associate pastor with prayer and with his presence, time, and money. He supported me when I was homeless. Sometimes I would refuse his assistance because I knew he too was struggling. Joseph is a humble man, but yet a stubborn man. He would refuse my refusal of his assistance. At the end of the day, Joseph always had his way because he believed in what he was doing.

Then there was also Tayo—so pure, so innocent, full of kindness and simplicity. Every adjective used here is truly descriptive of Tayo. At the time of our meeting, Tayo was going through a serious trial of her own. She always demonstrated that her trials were not about her and that there was a bigger picture that needed to be seen. I was soon attracted to this young girl who carried herself so confidently in spite of obstacles in her path. Tayo had faith. Faith attracts faith. Tayo and I began praying and seeing God overrun the enemy's camp in response to our cries in prayer.

One particular summer night of 2006 in the garage around two a.m., the Lord transported me to Benin City. Immediately in the spirit, I found myself in Benin City in around the year 2012. Benin had not made much progress, and God was saying that He had a preaching assignment for me to do there. The Holy Spirit showed me large crowds in Benin thirsty for the power of God that was lacking in their lives. This experience was repeated in a vision another night in the garage as I was about to open the elevator doors to do my round of inspection and inventory.

In 2005 and 2006, God had also shown me a series of visions especially concerning the church where I was associate pastor. At times, a spirit of prophecy would come upon me and I would prophesy openly in the church. To show that I was a workman approved in Christ, the Lord brought some of these prophecies to quick fulfillment. Others are still in the process of being fulfilled. The Holy Spirit was working in me and through me in ways I never imagined He would. I just was not worthy of this kind of thing. I felt that there were other people more holy than I was and that perhaps God had made a mistake. But God is perfect and so can never make a mistake. God knows why He chose to use me the way He was using me.

I also recall a certain vision the Lord gave me at a prayer meeting in the summer of 2006. In the spirit, I saw a moving bus with the name of a church inscribed on it. Passengers on the bus were fighting, and there was confusion. Because of the ongoing fight, a few passengers left the bus. When the fighting ceased, the bus started moving. When the passengers began to fight again, the bus would stop. The bus driver was going too slow even in the time of suspended fighting. I communicated this vision directly to the church leadership for prayer and resolution. A church somewhere was in trouble, perhaps ours, perhaps not. The purpose of this narration is not to expose the subject matter of the vision, but to show how God can work through His people. Suffice it to say that a few weeks later, the church experienced this turbulence as revealed and was able to come out in one piece by the grace of God.

I kept fighting my cause with the US Citizenship and Immigration Services and after much hassle, got my permission to work renewed. God had now stepped in. A few months later, my delinquent status in the New York State Bar was resolved. Now, I needed to raise money to pay my attorney registration fees and take some continuing legal education courses. The Lord God had reassured me that I would not have to beg for anything and that all I needed to do was to continue trusting Him. By December 2006, customers of the garage were showing exceptional generosity, and I accumulated sufficient tips to pay for my reinstatement into the New York Bar. A few months later, I secured a job as a contract attorney and enjoyed a dramatic rise in my income level.

The years 2005 and 2006 had seen me almost sifted as wheat. I had fled a bad marriage, leaving behind a lot of my personal effects, such as clothing and books. By the time I got the chance to practice law again, I had only two worn-out suits and four dress shirts, of which three were embarrassingly worn down. I alternated them on a daily basis. When I appeared for my first deposition hearing, the suit I wore looked like one worn since the 1960s. A Christian customer of the garage where I worked, Peter, who I mentioned earlier, had given me some beautiful ties. Wearing one of such beautiful ties on a worn-down suit only made my suit look even older. I promised myself that as soon as I got my first paycheck, I'd buy a suit and a nice dress shirt. God had provided a new income for me to meet my needs.

Man's inward character is revealed by how he handles the pressures of his trials. To God be the glory for giving me the grace to go through trials of homelessness, unemployment, hospitalization for partial heart failure, loss of property and friendships. Once you go through that you just come out wiser, humbler, and stronger. The Christianity today that preaches that suffering is not of God needs to be reexamined in the light of Scripture. In Philippians 3:10, Paul says, "I want to know Christ and the power of his resurrection and the fellowship of sharing in his sufferings, becoming like him in his death." In John 16:33, Jesus warns his disciples that trouble awaits them in the world and encourages them to take heart because he is in control. Christianity today, especially in America, is so scared of suffering. Many Christians are afraid of it and reject it even if the suffering is God's will for them. Christ's response to the agony He bore on the cross was for His father's will to be done. Many a time, in an attempt to evade a particular suffering, we end up outside the center of God's will. Little wonder many Christians are frightened when told to fast for a few days. It is always better to prepare for a day of crisis than to meet such a day unprepared. It can come like September 11—when least expected.

The life and trials of Job recorded in the book of Job, the eighteenth book of the Bible, is also quite significant. Society generally recognizes the attainment of adulthood to be age eighteen. If we can go through some of the things that Job went through without losing our cool, then we can claim not to be babies any longer. We can truly claim to be grownups in the faith. Chapter 1 of Job is sufficient for us to understand what Job endured. Here was a wealthy man who lost not only all his wealth but also all his children in one day. Fortunately, Job was a righteous man who did not lose one thing: his faith. In spite of all these overwhelming calamities, Job trusted in God. We see this illustrated more clearly in Job 1:20–22:

> At this, Job got up and tore his robe and shaved his head. Then he fell to the ground in worship and said: "Naked I came from my mother's womb, and naked I will depart. The Lord gave and the Lord has taken away; may the name of the Lord be praised." In all this, Job did not sin by charging God with wrongdoing.

When Job was at his Ground Zero, he did not blame God for his misfortunes. Neither did he forsake God as a result of feeling all was lost. Job maintained his faith in God throughout his gruesome ordeal. Remember, faith is the substance of things hoped for and the evidence of things not seen. Job's faith in God produced a manifestation of the substance of what he was hoping for. God rewarded Job by restoring unto him much more than what he had lost. It pays to trust in God. The difference between Job and the nation of Israel in Exodus is that the latter was always quick to grumble and complain when things did not appear to be working in its favor. It was quick to blame God and follow after other gods. This Israel had a predictable pattern. It rejoiced only when it saw goodies. Whenever it was tested by lack or delay, it always seemed to fail. It lacked the muscles of faith that constituted Job. An attribute of faith is perseverance. Faith that gives up is no faith at all.

Because God is a deliverer, a trial is but only a transition. It is a place of refining. Here, the debris we gather in life is sifted away to make room for a finer structure. It is not a place intended to be our destination. It is a place of transition and empowerment: transition to greatness and empowerment to serve.

Prayers of Deliverance

Meditate upon the following Scriptures: Psalm 68; Psalm 70; Psalm 118; Isaiah 47; Matthew 11:12; Luke 10:19; Mark 16:17–18; Romans 16:20; Ephesians 6:10–18; Galatians 3:13–14; Colossians 2:14–15; and Revelation 12:7–11. Be on a fast for seven days and pray loud and aggressively with all your heart the following prayers:

1. I present my entire being unto the Lord as a living sacrifice for cleansing through the blood of Jesus. In the name of Jesus, let the blood of Jesus cleanse me from every sin, curse, evil covenant, ungodly soul tie, and guilt.
2. I confess and repent of my sins and the sins of my ancestors in the name of Jesus.
3. I destroy with the blood of Jesus every demonic network operating against me. I command every devourer and waster of blessings in my life to depart now from my life in Jesus' name.
4. In the name of Jesus, I reverse the spells, incantations, pronouncements, and decrees of the enemy upon my life. I break the power of every curse and delay over my life and destiny in Jesus' name. I bind and cast out every spirit assigned to enforce a curse or

evil pronouncement in my life in the name of Jesus Christ.

5. I break the stronghold of marine witchcraft working against my life in the name of Jesus. I bind every spirit from the water keeping my blessings under the seas and rivers and command my blessings loosed and recovered in the name of Jesus.

6. In the name of Jesus, let the fire of the Holy Spirit enter into me and destroy every trace of darkness in me. Anything that the enemy has planted inside of me, whether visible or invincible, I command my body to reject it and eject it (vomiting, yawning, coughing, etc.) in the name of Jesus.

7. In the name of Jesus, I break the power of limitation and the spirit of stagnancy and failure assigned against me.

8. Every power denying the manifestation of God's promises in my life, God scatter them and destroy their works against me in Jesus' name.

9. Every strange spirit and stranger from darkness in my body, soul, and spirit, let the fire of God trouble them and chase them out in Jesus' name.

10. Every evil dedication of my life, I cancel and destroy you now in the name of Jesus. Evil altar manipulating my destiny, be destroyed by the fire of the Holy Spirit in Jesus' name.

11. In the name of Jesus and by reason of the anointing, I break every yoke of frustration and failure upon my life.

12. In the name of Jesus, I break and release myself from all demonic subjection to my ancestors and ancestral strong men that have dominated and controlled me.

10

Maintaining Your Deliverance

43 "When an impure spirit comes out of a person, it goes through arid places seeking rest and does not find it.

44 Then it says, 'I will return to the house I left.' When it arrives, it finds the house unoccupied, swept clean and put in order.

45 Then it goes and takes with it seven other spirits more wicked than itself, and they go in and live there. And the final condition of that person is worse than the first. That is how it will be with this wicked generation" *(Matt. 12:43–45).*

Getting deliverance is one thing. Maintaining it is another. When an impure spirit comes out of a person, it is deliverance. Upon its exit, the impure spirit goes through arid places seeking rest but does not find it. It seeks to return to its old abode in search of rest. Then it says, "I *will* return to the house I left"—the emphasis on "will" is mine. The word "will" demonstrates the evil spirit's firm determination to return to the house (the person) it was cast out from. Demons are always determined to return, and so we must be equally determined to keep them out and maintain the deliverance that we have received. Our deliverance is in and through Christ. The fact that Christ delivers does not mean that we can take our deliverance for granted. We are responsible for maintaining our deliverance.

Matthew 12:43–45 shows us the danger of keeping our vessels unoccupied after receiving deliverance. To avert this danger, we must receive proper spiritual counseling after deliverance. When the house is unoccupied, the evil spirit gets seven spirits more wicked than itself to return to the house. Since the house is unoccupied, there is no power there to resist their reentry. Now, the final condition of the person delivered is worse than the first because the house was left unoccupied instead of being filled with the presence and power of God. Jesus gives a verdict here. He says, "That is how it will be with this wicked generation." This present generation is even more wicked than the generation of two thousand years ago.

In these last days, mankind is progressing in the increase of wickedness and Jesus says the condition will be worse off for this generation. Why is this so? It is so because they sought deliverance and received it but refused to allow the deliverer space in their lives. Their houses were swept clean of demons, and they did not invite the Spirit of deliverance to abide in them. This is one reason many have received deliverance on one level or the other and have failed to maintain it. They have earnestly sought deliverance and not the Deliverer. They wanted their healing but were not willing to live in obedience to the Healer. Being delivered without developing a relationship with the Deliverer (the house is vacant) puts the person in a worse-off condition.

In order to receive and maintain your deliverance from evil powers, you must operate in the knowledge of certain truths. One of the greatest barriers to receiving deliverance is denial. Many are in denial that demons are in them. Until you come to a point where you recognize that there is a possibility that things other than your flesh are hindering your spiritual development, you cannot receive an enduring deliverance.

Knowing Who You Are in Christ

The first truth you need to appreciate is to know who you are in Christ. You are more than a conqueror in Christ Jesus *(Rom. 8:37)*. If you stand on the truth that you are more than a conqueror in Christ, no demon will be able to conquer you. Once you know who you are in Christ, you begin to do all to avoid sin and walk in holiness.

Zechariah 3:1–4:

> ¹ Then he showed me Joshua the high priest standing before the angel of the Lord, and Satan standing at his right side to accuse him.
>
> ² The Lord said to Satan, "The Lord rebuke you, Satan! The Lord, who has chosen Jerusalem, rebuke you! Is not this man a burning stick snatched from the fire?"
>
> ³ Now Joshua was dressed in filthy clothes as he stood before the angel.
>
> ⁴ The angel said to those who were standing before him, "Take off his filthy clothes." Then he said to Joshua, "See, I have taken away your sin, and I will put fine garments on you."

In Zechariah 3, Satan was resisting and accusing a priest ministering before the Lord. Satan was able to do this because the priest was dressed in filthy garments. Filthy garments represent sin. Sin gives Satan access into our lives to accuse and resist us. Sin attracts Satan and his demons. We must continuously confess and repent of sin. With the woman cut in adultery in John 8, Jesus restores her and instructs her to go, and sin no more *(John 8:11)*. There is a correlation between sin, disease, curses, and demonic oppression. To be demon free, we must not only receive deliverance, we must walk blamelessly before God.

Knowing who you are in Christ is fundamental to your maintaining your deliverance. You must know and agree with the Word of God regarding the deity of Jesus Christ: Matthew 16:16–17; John 10:30; Colossians 2:9; Hebrews 1:3; and Revelation 1:8. You must know why Jesus came to earth and why he returned to heaven. He came to die that we may have eternal life *(John 3:16)* and to destroy the works of Satan *(1 John 3:8)*. Jesus returned to heaven because he had completed his assignment on earth and he needed to send the Holy Spirit to be in us and with us that believe. Christ gave us something and someone. He gave us eternal life and the Holy Spirit. When we begin to walk in the consciousness of who we are in Christ, the Holy Spirit and the Word of God impart the mind of Christ unto us. To maintain deliverance, we must crucify the flesh and have an ongoing living encounter with the Holy Spirit. The Holy Spirit comes to make us Christlike and to give us the mind of Christ. A form of godliness that denies the power of godliness cannot sustain a deliverance. The more you are like Christ, the less room the enemy has to infiltrate and operate in your life.

You must also know and understand the spiritual power, authority, and weapons you have been given in Christ. Be strong in the Lord and in the power of His might. As you stand strong in Christ without yielding to compromise, the victories you have won in deliverance will be secure.

Do Not Be Ignorant of the Devil's Devices

To keep your deliverance, you must know who the enemy is and who he is not. You must know your enemy so that you do not end up fighting the wrong battles. It helps to also know your enemy's strengths and weaknesses. Demons are liars and tormentors. They are under the authority of Satan, the great deceiver and father of lies. Satan is the accuser in the midst of the brethren. He is the prince of the air. The enemy's major strength lies in deception. Demons want us to believe a lie as truth and the truth as a lie. The platform that enables deception to reign is ignorance. In this area, you cannot afford to be ignorant of the devil's devices *(2 Cor. 2:11)*. Satan's weakness is revealed when you are submitted to God and you resist him. Then, he flees *(James 4:7)*. As you plead the blood of Jesus and confess the Word of God, you will overcome powers of darkness *(Rev. 12:11)* in the name of Jesus.

You can only confess the word that you know. Begin a systematic study of the Bible and be in prayer always in order to build up your spiritual muscles and keep powers of darkness out of your vessel. In addition, keep ungodly soul ties cut off. These ties make you want to look back at some of the "good old times," and you must remain severed from them because they are demonic paths that Satan will seek to use to regain entry into your life.

Counseling

In the multitude of counsellors is safety *(Prov. 24:6)*.

When undergoing deliverance and subsequent to deliverance, it is critical for one to submit to righteous counseling. To maintain deliverance, you must be connected to the right spiritual covering and counsel. It will be difficult for Satan to devour someone who is alert and self-controlled *(1 Pet. 5:8)*. Counseling enables us to be alert in certain areas where we are prone to being vulnerable. Counseling probes the root problems that enable demonic activities and works to uproot them. Awareness is key. People perish for lack of knowledge *(Hosea 4:6)*. People must receive teaching on God's Word regarding their deliverance. The people going through deliverance must also be effectively counseled to change their habits and ways of thinking.

Whoever digs a pit may fall into it; whoever breaks through a wall may be bitten by a snake *(Eccles. 10:8)*.

As you seal every breach in your wall, the serpent will never get the opportunity to bite you and reintroduce poison into your life all over again.

Prayers to Maintain Deliverance

Meditate on the following Scriptures: Exodus 14:13; Psalm 24; Matthew 12:43–45; Galatians 2:20; James 4:6–7; and 1 Peter 5:8. Pray as follows:

1. In the name of Jesus, I cover my entire life with the blood of Jesus and put on the whole armor of God against the wiles of the devil.
2. Lord Jesus, baptize me in the Holy Spirit and give me a hunger and a thirst for Your Word that I may walk in the spirit and not in the flesh.
3. Heavenly Father, place a hedge of protection around me and send fierce warrior angels to guard me against demonic infiltration in the name of Jesus.
4. In the name of Jesus, I declare that every spirit of bondage that left me will never find me to be a resting place. Holy Spirit, overflow in me in Jesus' name.
5. In the name of Jesus, I declare that my body is a temple of the Holy Spirit, and I shall not be tormented or defiled by any evil power.
6. Holy Spirit, give me the mind of Christ and create in me a steadfast spirit that abides in the Word of God.
7. Lord, strengthen me in my inner man that I may stand against the wiles of Satan and walk in victory in the name of Jesus.

ABOUT THE AUTHOR

Idemudia Guobadia is pastor of Overcomers In Christ Faith Assembly in Brooklyn, New York and pastor of Overcomers In Christ Deliverance Assembly, Newark, New Jersey. He is a worker for Christ called to intense prayer intercession, spiritual warfare, deliverance of those under demonic oppression, evangelism, church planting, teaching and simplifying the Word of God, and preaching the gospel of Jesus Christ. He is also the author of *Working for Christ* and *Deeper Dimensions of Power.*

Made in the USA
Middletown, DE
22 May 2019